FRESH INK

Essays from
Boston College's
First-Year Writing
Seminar 2002

Edited by
Eileen Donovan-Kranz
AND **Lad Tobin**

**McGraw-Hill Primis
Custom Publishing**

Boston   Burr Ridge, IL   Dubuque, IA
Madison, WI   New York   San Francisco   St. Louis
Bangkok Bogotá Caracas Lisbon London Madrid
Mexico City Milan New Delhi Paris Seoul
Singapore Sydney Taipei Toronto

McGraw-Hill Higher Education

*A Division of The **McGraw-Hill** Companies*

FRESH INK
Essays from Boston College's First-Year Writing Seminar 2002

McGraw-Hill's Primis Custom Publishing consists of products that are produced from camera-ready copy. Peer review, class testing, and accuracy are primarily the responsibility of the author(s).

The opinions or views expressed in this work are those of the individual authors (of the essays) and do not necessarily reflect the opinions or recommendations of the editors of this work or Boston College.

1 2 3 4 5 6 7 8 9 0 BKM BKM 0 9 8 7 6 5 4 3 2

ISBN 0-07-285009-4
Editor: Ann Jenson
Manuscript Design and Preparation: Jakarta M. Eckhart, NiteOwl Creations
Photography: Toby Gordon
Printer/Binder: Book-Mart Press

Acknowledgments

Every summer for the past nine summers, Eileen Donovan-Kranz and I have published a new edition of *Fresh Ink*. What we've learned over those past nine summers is that all sorts of things can go wrong along the way and that, unless we get help from all sorts of generous and capable people, there will be no copies of *Fresh Ink* available when the first-year students arrive in August to buy their books.

This year those generous and capable people included all five members of our department's terrifically helpful, efficient and upbeat staff: Trese Ainsworth, Melissa Cote, Judy Plank, Jackie Skolnick and Angelica Wilshire. Judy called for papers and then, with Melissa, helped collect and collate the hundreds of essays that dribbled in throughout the exam periods in December and May. Angelica recorded all submissions. Jackie took care of all correspondence with the *Fresh Ink* authors. And Trese, an experienced FWS instructor and Assistant to the Chair, gave me useful advice on a wide variety of *Fresh Ink*-related matters.

We are fortunate, too, to be working again with a very talented, professional and accommodating team at McGraw-Hill: Ann Cady Jenson, our Custom Publishing Representative; Jakarta M. Eckhart, our production editor; Maggie Lytle, our cover designer; and Autumn Coleman, our sales representative. All of these people have gone beyond the call of duty to help us produce the book we imagined when we began sifting through the submissions last spring.

I want to give special thanks to Ricco Siasoco who generously volunteered to help us select the final essays and who read each of the submissions with tremendous care and thoughtfulness; to Emma Tobin who read all 398 submitted essays with great intelligence and compassion, and who made significant contributions during every phase of the editorial process; and to Toby Gordon, a talented artist with an eye for the telling detail, who gave us that wonderful photograph on the cover.

Of course, the 398 students who submitted essays were helped by the fifty-two extraordinarily dedicated and talented instructors who taught sections of the First-Year Writing Seminar in 2001-02: Jim Adams, Treseanne Ainsworth, John Anderson, Wayne Barr, Maria Brandt, Hilda Carey, Joanna Cook, Diana Cruz, Beth Dacey, Suzanne Davis, Andrea DeFusco, Joanne Diaz, Eileen Donovan-Kranz, Dacia Gentilella, George Grattan, Kathleen Hardiman, Elaine Healy, Diane Hotten-Somers, Rebecca Ingalls, Suzanne Johndrow, Jeffrey Jones, Christopher Kamerbeek, John Kulsick, Matt Lamberti, Colleen Lannon, Babo Leibovitch-Kamel, Skye Masson, Paula Mathieu, Jessica McGrew, Laura McIninch, Sarah Messick, Mike Michaud, Holly Moran-Bates, James Najarian, George O'Har, Jeff Ousborne, Nicholas Parker, Jacqueline Pena, Susan Roberts, Jamin Rowan, Erich Schliebe, Melanie Scott, Staci Shultz, Ricco Siasoco, Robert Stanton, Francis Storrs, Mary-Katherine Stouffs, Erica Sturtevant, Elaine Tarutis, Rebecca Troeger, Stephanie Tyburski and Jane Unrue.

Even with all of this noteworthy assistance, this book would not have come together if not for the contributions of Eileen Donovan-Kranz, whose uncommon skill as a teacher, writer and editor, is evident on every page of *Fresh Ink*; of our editor, Rebecca Ingalls, who once again demonstrated her remarkable ability to embrace contraries by making this book as consistent, correct and graceful as possible while still maintaining each author's original language and voice; and, most of all, of those 398 FWS students, who made sure that our time this summer was very well spent.

LT
June 2002

Table of Contents

Research, Inquiry and Documentation 97

Argument and Persuasion 129

Introduction

Many first-year writing programs allow students to produce only one kind of writing — analytic essays about assigned readings. When I asked the director of one of these programs why his students were never given a chance to choose their own topics, experiment with other forms of nonfiction or write from personal experience, observation and reflection, he gave me a patronizing look:

> "We've found that if you let college freshmen choose their own topics, they never challenge themselves with difficult topics or questions."

Before I could begin to respond, he went on:

> "When eighteen- or nineteen-year-olds try to write about a significant personal experience, they just don't have the maturity or perspective to craft a successful essay about it."

By that point, it was obvious to me that the guy didn't have a clue about what first-year students are capable of, and just as obvious that he hadn't had a chance to read the sort of essays that were submitted this year for publication in *Fresh Ink*. In fact, it is hard for me to imagine a better rebuttal to that writing program director's unfounded assumptions than this collection of essays. In a variety of forms and on a variety of topics, the writers of this ninth edition of *Fresh Ink* struggle intelligently and courageously with what it means to live in this world in this very uneasy time.

There are no "my most embarrassing moment" or "how I won the big game" essays here and, while there are some light-hearted moments, there are no lightweight thinkers. In fact, I should warn you: this year's edition is not an easy read. There are essays about the unspeakable deaths of beloved family members; about suffering in the streets of St. Petersburg and in the orphanages of Seoul; about World War II, Vietnam and 9/11; about the pain of living with obesity, clinical depression and a family history of Alzheimer's; about premature babies, homophobia, reincarnation, globalization, electroconvulsive therapy, a dangerous tropical storm, sexual assault, assault and battery.

But when I say that this year's edition is not an easy read, I'm not just referring to the "heaviness" of the topics; I'm referring to the complexity of thinking combined with the depth of feeling you will find in these essays. Taking on issues that clearly matter to them, these authors seek to answer questions that have no easy answers: how does the Boy Scouts' discrimination against gays affect Boy Scouts who are straight and non-homophobic? Is it unethical to eat meat? Should violent juveniles be tried and sentenced as adults? How can we resist xenophobia in the face of the fear and anger generated by the events of September 11th?

But while I mean to warn you, I do not mean to scare you off. While the authors of these essays take on unsettling subjects, each writes with a thoughtfulness and eloquence that offer the reader perspective, insight and hope. I also do not mean to suggest that *every* essay in this year's *Fresh Ink* is somehow about tragedy and loss and other *big* topics: in fact, there are wonderful pieces here about the surprising significance of small moments — about what it is like, for example, to hang out at a family potluck dinner in Brownsmead, Oregon; to attend a poetry slam in Central Square; to sit on a porch in Damascus, smoking a water pipe and listening to distant drumming; to be the kind of fourth grader who carried a briefcase instead of a backpack. Analyzing what most of us ignore or take for granted, one writer looks at why teenagers, like, use the word *like* so often. Another wonders what it means that most Americans seem no longer to value the penny. And a third analyzes Oliver Stone's technique by taking apart his film *JFK* frame by frame.

Whether trying to find language for the seemingly unspeakable or meaning in the seemingly insignificant, each of these essays demands to be read and shows just how much first-year students can accomplish when they are given the freedom and responsibility to write about what they think matters most.

Lad Tobin
Director of the First-Year Writing Program

Description

I

At the Cantab Lounge

Patrick Blair

"Let that inner poet in you wiggle its way out. Slam 'em with your best verses at the Boston Poetry Slam and Open Mic at the Cantab Lounge." This is what I read in *The Heights* last Wednesday while I was finishing my lunch. This one little sentence seemed to cut right through to my dissatisfaction with my experience so far at Boston College. I came here with the idea that it was the time when one "grows." I was told that college was when you found your loves, where your true passions lie. College, I thought, would be a chance to pursue those passions.

But so far, BC had been almost a repeat of my high school experience; the only difference was that now I was expected to manage my own time. I found high school completely devoid of *soul* — there was no passion that went beyond the weekend parties. School was tedious; no one was actually actively engaged. The teachers who had the power to inspire the students, to create an excitement around a subject and an interest to learn, were few and far between, and even these teachers were usually ineffective because the kids were too detached or too stoned to care, anyway.

That's why, when I saw the blurb about the Cantab Lounge Poetry Slam in *The Heights,* it occurred to me that here was an opportunity, a dare, to see if I could finally do what I had been complaining about. It's very easy to complain, but it's very hard to actually make a change. To understand how this innocuous little piece of text in *The Heights* affected me, one has to understand that I have a deep affection for literature, a love that seems to grow each year. I have this ridiculous dream of reading everything. It's an obsession rooted in two very important parts of my personality. First, I feel I have been sheltered my whole life and that I am looking to see what lies beyond

3

the suburbia that I grew up in. Secondly, I have my own goals of becoming a writer, but realize that I have a lot to learn before I can write anything meaningful.

This blurb in *The Heights* spoke to me that day. It played into my desires to take advantage of the experiences college was offering me, and it played into my love of literature. As I read about the Slam, questions started jumping around in my mind. Poetry Slam? What is that? Should I go? Is this going to be a yuppie crowd? Is this a touchy feely group thing? Is it going to be like a Starbucks? Well, I wasn't really about to go. I had class and I didn't want to have to explain to my roommate where I had been when I got back. But the idea stuck with me all day and when I came back to my room after class I took one look at my white-washed walls in my little box of a room, one look at my computer, and I ran like hell.

The Cantab Lounge is all the way over in Cambridge, so it took me over an hour to get there. When I got off the T I didn't really know what to look for. I still had the image of a coffee shop in my head. What I found instead was a bar. Blues music was blaring out from the inside. I was pissed. I came all the way over to hear poetry and it's in some bar, and you probably have to be twenty-one to enter. What a waste. But I wasn't going to turn around without a fight. Maybe they might let me in if I threw myself at their mercy, asked them to give me a mark on the hand or something so I couldn't get served.

When I walked in, my despair just increased. The Cantab Lounge was just a bar. Dirty and grungy, it reeked of cigarettes, and lonely people were scattered about. No one looked like a poet and the place certainly was not designed for a poetry reading. I let go of my male ego for a brief second while I asked a waitress where the poetry slam was being held. She said it was downstairs. Relief. Thank God. This could be all right, plus I hadn't even been asked for an ID yet.

Walking down those stairs was probably the wisest thing I have done since I have been at school. I didn't realize from that ad in *The Heights* that I was about to attend not a poetry reading, but *slam* poetry. I had figured the name was just a catchy term contrived to attract people. I had, sadly, never heard of slam poetry. I looked up the term online the next day and found that it is an off-branch of poetry, one that is based around audience participation. It's not a poetry reading, but a performance (everything is memorized): the *learn along with him.*

poet feeds off of the audience and the audience feeds off of the poet. To further crowd participation, audience members volunteer to be judges in the slam-off. A slam-off is a competition that is based around a series of head-to-head battles between two poets, with the best poet from each battle moving on to the next round until there are just two poets remaining. The winner of this final battle wins the entire competition. There are five judges. After a performance the judges show their scores. The highest and lowest scores are dropped, the remaining scores are added up and that is the poet's score. The highest score wins.

This particular evening featured an open mic, allowing anybody to sign up to read or perform a poem. But this part of the night was not necessarily slam poetry. The second part of the night included a guest slam-poet and the final part of the evening was the slam-off. The beginning of the night was a bit chaotic, quality-wise. The fact that anybody could come in and read poetry practically guaranteed that there would be some bad poems. One guy came up and read about dropping acid in a tunnel in college, and after about five performers in a row, I decided that the words *languid* and *sanguine* should be banned from all poetry for the rest of human existence. But the open mic had its high points, points when the poetry soared.

A good poet is able to draw you into intellectual battle, forcing you to question your beliefs and justify them along with the beliefs and thoughts of the poet. I don't know how to describe this without being too clichéd, but when this happens, everybody in the room soars with the poetry. The poets create poems where the words seem to gain a physical form. They come out and wrap the entire room in them. For that one poem the audience is living in the words, and the words allow everyone to transcend the room and to actually gain a glimpse of the author's mind. That night, every time such a poem ended, I felt that I was actually placed back in the Cantab Lounge, back in my seat. The poems were almost a rap; they revolved around the rhythm of the words, which, I think, is one secret to slam poetry.

The rhythm of the words drew you in and forced you to step in line. The only experience that I have had that was comparable to this night was being at a concert based around improvisation. The music draws you in and you start to move as the improvisation envelops you. For the duration of that song nothing else exists outside of the music; the rhythm moves you, and you and the band are involved in an exploration. The slam poetry did this, but it wasn't a physical experience, where the movement of the music carried you

reflection

away. Rather, it was an intellectual experience, where the words brought you to a different plane, an area beyond any physical existence.

As the night progressed the poetry only got better. The feature poet was a man named Michael Roosa, who had a self-proclaimed "unique technique to speak." He had poems about slavery, about love and about being a moral person in an environment that tends towards the amoral. Any disappointment I felt with the open mic section was soon forgotten as he weaved in and out of his poetry on the little wooden stage in the front of the room. After the feature poet was the slam-off, which, since it is based around the best poets continuing to perform, only got better and better.

The stories I heard here were completely beyond anything I had ever expected or heard in my life. There were no constraints on one's speech in this environment, something that was so foreign to me. In high school I had never heard any writing even the least bit controversial, except for maybe *Huckleberry Finn*, with its supposed racism. Here, though, the cuffs were off and anything went. I heard a story about a boy who had "queer" carved in his back by some football players because he was listening to Queen while studying, which left no one in the audience unmoved. I heard a story about a boy whose friend had killed himself and the connection the suicide shared with the incidents at Columbine. The most intense moment of the entire night was when one poet, who had never read or shared his poetry with anyone before, read a poem called "Everybody Wants to Be a Nigger."

None of these subjects would ever have been touched or discussed at my private high school. I had no idea that poems like these were out there, nor did I know how relevant they could be. Issues which should be discussed (but are usually swept under the rug at most of the institutions I have known) were presented openly. The poetry slam served me with a wake-up call to the sheltered life I have lived and continue to live here at BC. I came away from this night feeling more free, more a part of life, than I had ever felt before, and therein lies the magic of my first night at the Cantab Lounge.

Brownsmead, Oregon
(25 minutes east of Astoria)

Adrian Anderson

Zoe's parents drove a gray Corolla from the '70s. Rust, like a resilient plant, thrived in the car's seams. Brownish-golden lichens grew from the cracks along the tops and bottoms of the doors, where they tucked themselves underneath the vehicle.

Zoe's dad used the car to haul wood from the other side of town for their fire. Wedges of white wood thrown into the back seat, which was always folded down flush with the base of the hatchback trunk, caused hundreds of slivers to become snagged in the scratchy black surface, resembling, by feel and function, Velcro. Also strewn in the back were chunks of bark that had peeled off and been left. Some were big and warped like half cylinders and some had moss on them. The air in the car was heavy and earthy. It smelled like wood. Zoe smelled like wood and smoke — wet wood and sometimes cedar. It was in his hair.

Something about the back of the car was comfortable to Zoe and me; it was our fort, regularly including a spider or large black ants. It was a place where we played for hours and, as we would later admit, the place where we thought and grew. As adolescents, we'd lie on our backs with our legs dangling over the rear bumper and talk about girls and school and drugs.

However, on this day Zoe and I were crawling around with matchbox cars under our palms, making *vroom* noises and collision sounds. Zoe's parents were sitting quietly in front. Zoe's mom sat in the passenger seat, hugging a giant bowl of potato salad she had made for the potluck. Her beige dress seemed to glow faintly in the dark interior. As the morning progressed and the day became green and bright we would roll the windows down and let summer in.

We drove north along Highway 101 under dark corridors of over-hanging trees, blinking through slender rays of light that lay across the road, until the Columbia slid out into the Pacific and the river severed our path. At a stoplight, Zoe and I stopped playing for a moment and sat up to look out the windows at the river's giant mouth. The intersection of the ocean and the Columbia is wild and immeasurable, highlighted by swirling water and short, sharp, white-capped swells created by the wind that even on the calmest days funnels in from the Pacific and whips and gusts up the Columbia Gorge all the way to Portland. The line where the two bodies of water meet looks like a two-foot-high mountain range running from shore to shore. It was this that I looked at whenever I was near the river. This division, as far as I could tell, was a physical constant, yet no explanation, no matter how scientific, ever satisfied my curiosity. The line was a constant in me. I often thought about it. I imagined the force of the water and tried to realize it by pushing my hands together as hard as I could in front of my chest. My arms shook, but never moved. I pushed until they hurt and I was tense and tired. I wanted to know why the Columbia and the Pacific were so opposed to one another and why they protected themselves so rigidly.

On the far side from where our car sat idling, across the expanse of rough water, apparently flawless hills textured with thousands of turquoise blue-green trees rose from the river's shore. A single stoplight in the center of the small three-way junction, suspended by cables, swayed in the wind. The light turned green. The rear of our car sank in acceleration. We turned away from the coast and drove fast along the curvy two-lane highway above the Columbia.

Eventually, we left the highway onto a small road. After a mile the road turned to dirt, and after another mile it wasn't a road at all, but a drive-way, leading to a farm.

The potluck was on this farm. Rectangular tables borrowed from the schoolhouse were set in the grass behind the barn. Parked cars bordered the dirt driveway, some resting at an angle into the ditches on each side of the road. On the tables was food: five salads, sandwiches, eggs, smoked fish, oys-ters, cheeses and crackers, beer, juice, homegrown vegetables, blackberry pie and apple pie. A group of adults was sitting in a circle, turning the crank on an ice-cream maker. There were bare feet and men with no shirts. This was how Zoe lived. Everyone's hair smelled like his. The atmosphere was sweet. It tingled my nose. I thought about the mouth of the Columbia again, how it is always shifting and constantly deceiving even itself, and how huge tankers with red hulls became stranded on sandbars and beat apart by the waves. I remembered watching seagulls trying to fly along the river, flapping their wings, dipping and rising and being pushed back by the wind. I remembered the different colored currents swirling in every direction. My stomach was making me dizzy. I wanted to be cool and refreshed. I wanted to lie under the sun and dissolve into the ground, to be part of it.

We ran and played tag with the other kids. Zoe's mom chased us for a while, purposely moving slow, stiff-armed and giant-like, until we collapsed from exhaustion after laughing and shrieking and gasping for air. She hugged us both at once and told us we were beautiful.

Later, Zoe and I sat in the shade under the tables while Zoe's dad, who never talked much, played his guitar. He stopped only when the pipe being passed around the circle was held out under his nose. He took it, smoked and played more, and the people sitting with him hummed and rocked on their hands.

I was still light-headed and felt empty-stomached. I wanted to drink water or even dunk my head in it. Cold water. I thought that soon I'd black out. "Let's go sit with them," Zoe said of the people sitting in the music circle. I told him that I didn't want to and, indeed, I didn't want to, but my hesitancy was unexplained. I would refuse, yet I wasn't truly content there, under the table. Perhaps the river didn't know why it fought the Pacific, either.

We listened in silence while pulling fistfuls of grass from the ground until Zoe crawled out from under our table and I followed, the tablecloth sliding over our heads and along our backs until we stood up and sprinted away from the food and people to the farthest corner of the lawn. I was behind Zoe, pursuing as fast as I could. Under a tree, where the grass was sparse and the soil was wet and cool on our feet, we stopped. I stayed there when Zoe ran off again. Maybe it was because I was tired, but probably because the ground was fresh and comfortable. So I sat down and pushed my thumb on the ground and a little pool of cool brown water came up. I smiled. For a brief moment I wanted to stay under the tree forever.

Desperate St. Petersburg

Carl Smith

As I looked out of the bus window, I could see walls of once-mighty stone being held up by broomsticks. On the Mercedes-brand bus I felt safe from what I saw. The city was like a zoo, contained behind iron bars, where I was observing an exhibit from a distance. Potholes rocked the sturdy bus back and forth like a kayak in white rapids. The streets were so poorly maintained that the bottom-most layer of gravel was exposed in various areas. Somehow the driver was able to maneuver through the labyrinth of roads.

I was on a cruise that made a two-day stop in Russia along its tour of the Baltic. Like cattle, our group of sightseers moved from sight to sight and store-to-store. For the majority of the trip we were kept on a bus with a tour guide. The Russians were intent on keeping us off the streets as much as possible. The first morning, our guide, in brilliant tone of voice, called St. Petersburg "the Jewel of the East." She was a surprisingly well-fed woman whose ringing voice could be heard at either end of the bus. Her clothes were slightly battered and her hair was unkempt. The woman looked as if she had been working for three straight days without a break. Although she was convinced that St. Petersburg was the most exquisite city in the world, our guide did not hesitate when describing the poverty. "The average wage here is about one hundred dollars a month," she exclaimed. Shortly after the statement I could hear mumbling among the shocked tourists. St. Petersburg, the highlight of Russia, sharply contrasted with the plush three- or four-bedroom homes to which almost every passenger on the cruise had grown accustomed.

The city is highly centralized, with a river running through the middle of it. Buildings, prisons and markets line the shore. Walking along the edge, I made the mistake of looking into the river. The water was putrid. A memory of my family's leaking septic tank suddenly came to mind. I could feel whatever was producing that wretched scent beginning to cling to my clothes and nose. People were actually out in the river with their boats. How they could withstand the sight and smell of the waste that they drove through? Paper cups, cigarette butts, bags, clothes, food, gasoline and small rodents gave the river its bizarre aroma. The toxic mixture produced a color I had never seen before. It was olive with a black tint that slightly outweighed the green. A teacher once taught me that a body of water gets its color by reflecting the sky. Apparently there are exceptions.

Our tour guide pointed out almost every single structure that had any importance in the city. What appeared to be low-end apartment buildings were actually government offices and museums. The beautiful brick and stone that once shined with luster were crumbling apart into dust. Paint chipping off the walls only revealed a layer of cheap cement that had been used to plug up the numerous holes. A prison stood tall among the shattered skyline. That was probably the only building that absolutely needed to be kept intact. The last citywide renovation must have occurred in 1712, when Peter the Great originally built it.

Watching grand buildings crumble became a memory after I saw the people of the city. On the second day of my stay in St. Petersburg, the guide took us to a public market. At a first glance it seemed like any European setup. Rows of shops were lined up neatly, with a couple of employees attending each stand. Every city I had previously visited on the trip had this feature. I was therefore not surprised at first. Only after I stepped off of the bus did I want to leave Russia as soon as possible. At the sight of potential shoppers, all of the employees came out from behind their shops and assembled themselves in a row. The men stood straight up and smiled at us kindly while the women propped their arms close together as to show us their breasts. My heart sank and I could feel my knees beginning to weaken. The workers looked like orphans, showing themselves off, hoping that they would be selected to receive a home. As I walked along the shops, each woman I passed gave me a seductive "hello" and a smile. They were desperate. Most of the items for sale were the same. Clothes, papier-mâché boxes and old communist memorabilia. One man tried to sell me an old Soviet pilot's suit, complete with a helmet and oxygen mask. It took nearly 10 minutes to convince him that I was not going to fly a fighter jet any time soon. I stood far away from the crowd until it was time to leave. I was ashamed. The stand owners, all adults, cowered to the group as if to acknowledge some form of inferiority. They were willing to do anything for just one American dollar.

The pathetic scene only worsened when the tour bus stopped at the Hermitage. Upon opening the doors, our guide had to push away the peddlers plugging the doorway. She told us specifically not to make eye contact with any of them. As I exited the bus a man sat in front of me. He had lost his legs and didn't have a wheelchair to move him. When the man saw me he put some merchandise into his mouth and crawled to where I was standing. He could not speak English but rather just stared at me. The sun forced him to squint. A bright glare exposed the dirt and sweat that covered his face. In his mouth was a bag with a collection of nesting dolls. Most of them were painted with stars and stripes. Others resembled U.S. presidents. The last things I wanted to buy in Russia were patriotic American trinkets. A tear began to swell in his eye. Trying to escape the mob, I ran into the Hermitage as fast as I could. A Rembrandt painting faced me as I entered. It was beautiful.

Narrative

15

At Home in a Foreign Land

Tara Lynn Mechrefe

I felt someone tugging at the leg of my pants and anxiously jerked my head around. At first I thought that no one was behind me, but then I looked down at the ground and noticed the eyes of an older woman piercing through the sea of black cloth that surrounded both her face and body. Her dark black eyes were accented by a thick line of black eyeliner that made them even more pronounced and persecuting. I could not figure out what I had done wrong. She was clearly distraught about something, but would not say anything to me. She just kept tugging at me and pointing out into the masses of cloaked women with a finger from her worn hand — each crease on her palm was dark and deeply embedded into her skin. I looked at her with worried eyes and then surveyed the crowd again. My eyes darted around the open room. All that I could see were women crouched down and hunched over in bundles of black cloth. From each corner of the swarming waiting room unwelcoming eyes were shooting glares at me from behind their massive *chadors*.

I grabbed at my sister's side, and asked her what we were supposed to do. She was just as puzzled as I was and had no answer for me; she simply shrugged her shoulders and looked back at me with the same nervous eyes that I wore.

My cousin, Nouhad, was up ahead at a counter near the entrance of the mosque, where a man was collecting everyone's shoes. She was receiving instructions from a man who resembled most of the men there — the classic Middle Eastern look. His face was confidently exposed — masked by nothing — and his eyes had the same penetrating effect. His skin looked how mine would look if I had placed my hands into the dusty dirt that covered their land and rubbed it deep into the pores of my own skin. His small mustache twitched from side to side as he barked the directions in Arabic to my docile cousin. I watched as Nouhad quickly nodded her head, afraid of upsetting him by even questioning him once.

☙

We had arrived in Damascus only three days before. I had been completely overwhelmed by my surroundings. The land looked exactly as I had seen it depicted in various movies. My parents had attempted to describe it to me, but I would have never imagined it to look as though it actually were a different world, a third world. The buildings are all shapeless brown and grey mounds of concrete, with people constantly rushing into, out of and around them. The streets are overcrowded and overpowered by men. During the day you see women walking about the car-infested streets; however, these women do not really look like women. Rather, they look like shapeless, black, floating figures — figures usually grasping onto the hands of their children, fearing that if they let go of their hands for even one minute they will be run over by the wanton drivers. It is a city where the pedestrians mean nothing. If you are in the street, you are in the territory of the cars, and they will not slow down for you to cross the street. Instead, they will speed up and beep so that you fearfully jump back onto the dilapidated curb. However, only during the day do you even get to see these black ghosts wandering the streets, for at night they recede back into their homes and wait until daylight to emerge once again.

I never imagined that I would feel this way when I entered the homeland of my parents. This is their country, their heritage, their home. But is it, really? The people here look different from my family; it is as though their animosity towards ancient enemies is constantly on their minds, running through their veins. I feel as though they look at me and think: outsider. I feel as if people are just waiting for the moment when they can steel my pocketbook or pull some sort of scam on me — just because I have that "deer caught in headlights" expression plastered on my face.

☙

The four of us walked into the dusty street and immediately spotted the relatively new turquoise Honda Civic among the masses of many decrepit cars parked there. Nouhad turned around from the driver's seat and informed us that it would take nearly a half an hour to get to the mosque. I was not bothered by this because we had been bored all afternoon, anyway. As she began to pull out, Nabil turned around and asked us if we had remembered our scarves. My sister and I both answered him in unison, as we held them up for him to see.

As we departed the city, the hustle and bustle was also left behind. We were driving through desert-like land — no plants, no people, just emptiness. Occasionally, we would pass bands of men walking along the road. I could tell from way their usually rich, tan skin appeared dull that they were covered in the dust that lingered in the air.

As we approached our destination, the streets began to fill with more people. Every single woman was covered by thick garbs; usually there were some uncovered women interspersed, but not here. I could tell that my cousins were beginning to get nervous, for they had both never been here, and were not sure where the mosque was located. Nouhad needed to ask for directions, but was very hesitant. She finally rolled down her window and gestured to a man standing on the curb. As he walked over to our suspicious car, I noticed Nabil tucking his cross behind his shirt. The man peered inside and saw that none of our heads were covered. After the man reluctantly gave us vague directions, Nabil thanked him and we drove off in search of the mosque.

※

"Put it on. Put it on now." Nouhad looked at me through worried eyes and I could see her hands trembling as she shoved the thick black cloak into mine. "Cover up. Cover your neck, your hair, everything."

"What is going on? What did the man at the counter say to you?" I answered back.

"Don't speak. Not in English or Arabic," she quickly whispered to me in Arabic. "They'll be able to tell."

She was struggling to tuck in all of the pieces of her hair. It was too short to be pulled back with an elastic band, so she had pieces falling out from behind the flower printed scarf on her head. She was about to answer me when she felt a woman on the floor yanking at the black *chador,* which was dragging on the floor from being so large.

"What? What is it?" Nouhad anxiously snapped back to the woman in Arabic. The woman would not answer her, she just kept pointing to her face. I could tell that my cousin was beginning to get frustrated as chunks of her hair, now damp from her perspiration, kept falling into her eyes. However, the mysterious woman on the floor was relentless and insistently pointed at her to hide them. Hide the hair. Hide the pieces of hair that would entice all of the men walking by: hungry men just hoping to get a glimpse of female flesh, or even better, hair. I could not understand their rationale — they forbid their women to reveal their hair or skin, but allow them to show off their eyes. To me, it seems as though eyes are the most seductive feature of a woman — especially the eyes of *these* women. Women who are stuck, trapped behind not only layers of clothing but also behind an amazingly evident dominant force: man.

It is four in the morning, and I am lying on the floor of my aunt's flat — giggling with my cousin, Nabil, as we chat about each other's crushes. Even though he is four years older than I, I feel like he is one of my best friends. Every summer he comes to visit the States we manage to stay up into the early hours of the morning, talking about absolutely nothing. For a minute, I forget where we are, and think that I am lying in the family room of my own house. Then we hear it. The remote hum from the loudspeakers perched on telephone poles on almost every other block. We look out the window and see the neon green lights that illuminate the sleeping city. Each light indicates a mosque, from which the Moslem prayer is being recited. Over and over the prayer goes — the hum of the man's voice not only fills the empty streets, but also the quiet homes. My cousin looks at me, then at his watch, and smiles.

"I guess it's time to pray." We both laugh. He gets on his knees, starts to bow up and down and recites the prayer, singing it in the same drone that I can hear echoed outside. He knows it by heart. We have already heard it five times today; maybe this makes six.

"What are they saying? What could possibly be this important to wake everyone up at four in the morning?"

"Well, they're basically reminding everyone that they are great, Allah is great and the Jews are the enemy."

I lie down again on the soft Persian rug and think about what he has just told me. I cannot comprehend.

I could feel the warmth of my own breath as I breathed through the thick material that covered my body; their uniform had transformed me from a woman into a shapeless object. I was merely a pair of eyes now, but still not like theirs. The minute we stepped inside the mosque I felt like I had been hit by a wave of heat radiating from the masses of bodies crammed inside. As I looked to the other side of the shrine, separated by a short fence, I saw Nabil among the crowd of praying men. The women were kept completely separate from the men, for men's prayers should never be distracted by anything — especially not by a woman. The swarming cloaks pushed and shoved their way through the throngs of people, never giving a friendly look, not even once. They were on a mission. Everyone was; and no one would tolerate anyone who came between him and his prayers.

I looked up away from the blackness and was completely astonished by the gleaming gold ceilings of the mosque. Intricately handcrafted carvings covered not only the ceilings, but the walls, as well. Everything that was not solid gold was painted with gold leaf and other rich colors. There were mirrored mosaics completely covering the tomb of the cherished St. Zanoub.

Through tears, many of the woman were tearing off pieces of bread and rubbing them all over the tomb, doing everything in their power to get as close as possible to the essence of their sacred prophet. They were all mumbling prayers that I could not even begin to understand, and after being in there for less than ten minutes, I felt the need to get out. I simply needed to escape from the madness that was thriving inside their sanctuary.

The aroma of the freshly ground Turkish coffee beans fills my nasal cavity — it soothes me as the smell travels down to my stomach. I love waking up to this smell. I love hearing the boisterous voices of my mother and her sister as they start off their day with the latest family gossip.

I walk into the small but cozy kitchen and give my aunt and mother the customary two kisses, one for each cheek. They invite me to sit down and have a cup of the strong coffee to wake me up. I accept the offer despite the fact that, to me, each sip tastes like ground-up tablets of aspirin. I find it strange that I would be perfectly content to smell that heart-warming scent all day long, yet I have trouble finishing the porcelain doll-sized cup.

I decide to make the process as painless as possible and finish it in one quick shot. I then tip it over, and prepare to have my fortune read through the dark mud-like coffee grind that drips along the pure white walls of the cup. Each time, a unique pattern is created so that no two cups can ever be read the same way. I try to sneak a quick look at the cup and cannot make any sense of what I see — my aunt then grabs it from my hand and gives me a look that says, "You will never make any sense of it, so don't even bother." Her face then cracks into a smile as she begins to unfold my fortune.

🌺

The minute we left the building, I felt the urge to rip off the *chador* that engulfed me. It was about ninety-seven degrees outside and the intense sun seemed to be burning a hole into me. Nouhad motioned to me to not remove it just yet. We brought the cloaks back to the counter and retrieved our shoes — I felt as though I were handing in my uniform, therefore symbolizing to them that I did not have what it takes to truly belong to their clan. I did not care. I did not want to belong. I longed to go back to where my family was; I could not bear to be disparaged any longer.

🌺

I blew the flavorful smoke out of my mouth, trying to form the cloudlike puffs into circles. I could not help but to giggle, which only made me choke on the smoke. I looked over at Nabil as he blew the smoke out of his nose, trying to look seductive. We both burst into uncontrollable laughter.

Smoking the *arguileh* here had definitely become what I enjoyed most. The Middle Eastern water pipe was something that everyone here smoked; it was the most relaxing thing that I had encountered in the country. As we sat on the porch and overlooked the city, I realized what I liked about it. I felt deep down inside that this was my true home — it is where my family lives, where my cultural pride originated, and it is the place my parents call home. I took a deep breath in, and felt the rose-flavored tobacco glide from my mouth deep down into my body. I tilted my head back and exhaled while watching the smoke flow fluidly through the air. I watched it sail away and eventually dissipate into the immensely beautiful black sky. I could hear the lull of distant drumming — people celebrating someone's return from Mecca. At that moment I knew that I would never be able to feel this way anywhere else, nowhere else would I be able to actually feel the surrounding culture. As I inhaled deeply I felt the rose flavor saturate my body. For a moment, I felt a pang of anxiety, but as I released the thick and curving smoke, it also escaped my body and mind.

meaving
condensation

Love, Peace and Happiness

Gina Chung

why present tense?

You step off of the plane and realize that you truly are alone. No mother, no father, no brother to watch over you. Part of you is happy about that, but most of you is sad that they sent you far away because they say that you, at age fifteen, are out of control. They keep repeating that you are only going to be working for the summer. They tell you that they love you and that they hope you come back a changed person. You nod, you pack and you leave, telling yourself repeatedly that this is for you. That's all you can do. When you find out that you need to take the bus from the Seoul International Airport all the way to the orphanage by yourself, you are on the verge of tears but drag your bags to the bus stop just the same.

The air smells like sweat, and the heat rolls off in beads down your face. You board the bus, taking the seat in the front so you can be as close to the exit as possible. After thirteen sleepless hours on the plane, you are in no condition to be sightseeing. The bumping and grunting of the bus strangely rocks you to sleep, and an hour later, you are awakened by a rough tap on your shoulder. At first, you don't remember that you're in Korea, on your way to work in an orphanage run by nuns. You think you're at home, that your mother is shaking you awake, so you slap her hand away and tell her to leave you alone.

Then, you remember where you are and snap awake. Grabbing your bags, you give the man who woke you up a dirty look. Hearing someone mutter something about ungrateful teenagers, you make as much noise as you can, getting off as slowly as possible. You look around and you stand there in front of the building, ready to bolt if someone comes out. Wild ideas race through your head. Actually, they are more stupid than wild. Maybe you could run off, leave your bags, somehow get back to the airport, trade in your ticket and fly back home. Yes, they are definitely stupid ideas. You sigh and head in.

You tell the first nun you see that you are the girl from America who is here to work for the summer. She nods and shows you to your room. It's a little bit cooler inside, so you are able to breathe better. There are cutouts of flowers and happy kids all over the walls. The halls are dimly lit, and through slightly open doors, you can catch glimpses of children everywhere. But these aren't normal children. They can't walk and they can't talk. They are slumped on the floors, in wheelchairs and in baby carriers. You think bitterly that the cutouts of flowers and happy kids don't seem to be helping these children any.

The next morning, the same silent nun motions for you to follow her. You learn that there are three sections to the orphanage, and they are named Love, Peace and Happiness. She stops at Happiness and tells you very softly to go in. So you do. And inside, there are so many children. None of them can walk or talk. You begin to notice that not all of them are children. There's a grown man sitting in a wheelchair in the corner, and he is slapping and gnawing on himself.

Days pass by, and you start to get used to it here. You have a daily ritual set up by now. You get up at eight, go to Happiness, stay with the children all day; at night, you walk down the long hallway back to your bedroom. You bathe under the faucet hanging from the wall in your bathroom, wash your clothes with soap and hang them up to dry next to your window. You sleep, tossing and turning in your blankets on the cold cement floor. You dream dreams full of Love, Peace and Happiness.

There is a little boy who is eight years old. But he cannot walk because his legs are not formed. So he crawls around on the floor, zapping around like a little tadpole. This child has a way of wiggling into your heart like no other person before. He zaps back and forth across the floor, and when he tries to eat a sock, you chastise him. You are trying very hard to hide your smile that is creeping up your cheeks. But you can't help the burst of laughter that comes out, so you just let it all go. You laugh and laugh, and the boy coos and giggles.

A month passes by, and you realize that the walk from your room to Happiness is too long. You decide, instead, to lie with the children all night long, staying with them while they cry and dream and sleep. You do the same.

There is a man there who is twenty-three years old. He is not really an orphan but he lives at the orphanage, anyway. You find out that his parents are very rich, that they are two of the richest people in Korea. But they do not want to take care of him. You meet his parents when they come to visit him. They speak, not to you, but in your direction, as they say that they would take him home if he would only recognize them, if he would only show a sign that he knew they were his parents. You know they are lying because even you can see that when they come, he stops slapping and gnawing on himself. When they come, he stops crying and starts smiling. He can't talk, but he doesn't need to talk for you to know that he is happy. So you give his parents a glare and go on with your work.

Your departure comes at you like a cement wall against your face. You don't want to leave. When they tell you that they have called a taxi for you, that you don't need to take the bus again, you thank them and walk mechanically down the hallway to your room. You gather your things; you don't have much to gather. You fold the blankets they provided you with on your first night, put on your backpack and drag your suitcase to Happiness. You kiss all of the children one by one, crying the entire time. You go down the stairs and out the door, leaving Happiness behind you with all its blessings.

You step off the plane and realize that you are truly glad. No Love, no Peace, no Happiness to watch over you. Part of you is sad, but most of you has realized that this is it. This is why they sent you away. You know you have not completely changed. But you see that somewhere along the line your perspective shifted somehow. You can't quite pick out the moment this happened — maybe it was the first time a child looked at you trustingly while you changed his diaper, or maybe it was when he held out his arms to be picked up — still, you know that it happened. You look around the terminal and smile when you see your parents and your brother. They stare at you, not quite sure what to do, and so you walk over to them and nudge them towards the door, to the car. You climb in and you head home, instantly falling into a dreamless sleep in the back of your father's gray Ford.

Baby Lessons

Nora Kaleshian

why if dies?

"Baby Brown," as the nurses refer to him, is going to have surgery today and is not allowed to eat, so of course he is fussy. He needs to be held. Before draping the sterile cotton shirt over my body and tying it behind my back, I remove the plastic hospital ID badge from around my neck. I sit down in the rocking chair and hold the five-pound, six-week-premature infant close to my body. Knowing that I am a fascinating object to him, I bring my face closer to his and smile. He stops fussing and stares back, and I am amazed at how well his eyes are focusing. An intravenous needle is placed in an arm slightly bigger than a man's thumb. He closes his eyes for a moment, and I am startled because his eyelids are so thin, almost transparent. I gently say his first name, Mathew, which is written on the plastic crib he sleeps in. These healthier babies are said to mature faster through human contact, so I touch his bare skin and sing to him.

Standing in a sunlit section of the large unit, I gaze at the tiny swaddled forms around me, each nestled in an incubator or crib of its own. I am in the Newborn Intensive Care Unit at Brigham and Women's Hospital in Boston, and volunteering here during the summer has become a significant part of my life. By dividing my time between the Department of Newborn Medicine and the actual unit, I have learned what it takes to care for a premature infant from the technical side, and what it is like to be face-to-face with a doll-sized human being.

For a moment, I think of how much I had wanted to get inside this unit and the red tape I had to plow through to achieve my goal. When I first began volunteering, I was placed in a stuffy office in the Department of Newborn Medicine, doing my supervisor's work. Each day, as I transferred information into the nurses' personnel folders, I dreamed about and schemed ways of actually getting to see the babies. When my supervisor asked me to place documents in the Policy, Procedures and Guidelines manuals, generally called the PPGs, I rejoiced at the chance to actually get inside the unit. Each time I finished the assigned job, I would linger in the A and D sub-units, where the healthier babies are located, and I would ask the nurses if they needed help. At first, they were suspicious and dismissed me; hospital bureaucracy does not allow volunteers to be in the unit. It did not matter; I kept coming back, introducing myself cheerfully over and over again when they forgot my name. Gradually, the nurses became accustomed to my presence and began asking me to hand things to them. Then one magnificent day a bald baby was placed in the crook of my arm, with his bird-like legs extending to my wrist. I was in heaven.

Holding Mathew for the first time, I feel content and yet protective of the small being whose life depends upon my care. Because babies can feel anxiety, I remind myself to stay calm. With his thin body wrapped in a baby blanket, I stare with amazement at the two tubes extending from his minuscule nostrils to the portable oxygen tank near my feet. I sing to him in a mixture of English and Armenian, using Armenian lullabies my mother sang to me, to calm his mewing noises. With his head in the crook of my arm and his toes extending to my wrist, I know that there is a chance that this miniature person will not survive, and the thought penetrates my heart to the core.

I refuse to accept that just because life and death are constant occurrences for the staff, and it is their duty to give the infants the best possible chance for life, that they must also be emotionally uninvolved. Even at less than one pound, all of the infants are lucky because they have dedicated staff and the newest medical technology. The doctors and nurses would not be there if they were anything but dedicated. They do not do this job for the money, however much they might earn.

The nurses especially hold the most heart-wrenching position because they are the ones who are with the infants day and night. They feed the babies with tiny bottles filled with special fortified milk, and try to get them to suckle on the even tinier nipples. They change their diapers, bathe them and insert needles into bony feet. The nurses are the ones who embrace crying babies when there is just not enough time.

I have seen the courage of medical personnel doing their utmost to save premature infants so precariously balanced on the roller coaster of life. I have seen a nurse cradling two babies at a time, trying to feed one while the other faintly cries. I have seen healthier preemies wide awake in their cribs, ready to be picked up, but not enough nurses available to hold them. In a place where tiny patients are so ill, I know I am crucial. This knowledge makes me realize my position in life and how close I am to choosing what I will do with my future. Fulfilling my potential duties here, the effects could be psychologically devastating, whether I stay ten years or one. I do not know if I can become a nurse and watch helplessly as some babies die and others live. Yet I am irreversibly drawn to this place.

Over the weeks, I watch Mathew's tiny face and body grow, and I am overcome with gratitude. Daily, he shows me that persistence can bring complete satisfaction. One month later, I place baby Mathew in his crib for the last time. The following day, he goes home. And I return again the next day, hoping a similar fate will come to another baby.

Signed in Red

Emily Stanger

It was black.

"**U**se the pot with the black rim; it has the caffeine. And keep the coffee black." I repeat Dad's words in my head as I walk down the long intimidating hallway. Of all the times I have been to the office with Dad, I have never been sent down it alone. We had traveled down the hallway together to launch our paper airplanes down three floors to the lobby, to get Cokes and coffee from the break room, or to find the receptionist's desk with the Jolly Ranchers, but I felt so old and important as I was sent on a solo mission for the first time. I was off to fill Dad's mug with the coffee he drank so quickly. It always seems as though he is ready for another cup. In fact, sometimes he will even fill two mugs at a time to bring back to his desk. I can remember him teaching me how to make coffee at home, how to scoop out those coarse grains that always smelled so good, and exactly how much to place in the white filter. It felt like such a big responsibility to make the coffee in the morning, as it was as important to Dad as brushing his teeth. Every morning he started out with his travel mug for the drive to work, filled to the brim with strong black coffee. For some reason I had always admired that quality in Dad, the fact that he didn't need any milk to go with his coffee like Mom did. It made him tough and respectable. And now today I am his secretary, making sure to keep his cup full. I grip the black-rimmed pot and slide it out of the machine. My hand shakes from the weight as I try to carefully pour it into his mug. I fill it to the rim, as nothing else will be added, and I slowly proceed back down the hall with both hands gripped tightly around the goods. As I smell the strength of the coffee, I look at the liquid and think of Dad taking a sip of the blackness and being pleased with my delivery.

�※

Deep down I knew there was trouble ahead as soon as I agreed to spend the evening with Amy. But I didn't listen, and it was ignoring those instincts that had gotten me into the situation. As I sat in the back bedroom, there was a haze over my mind and a discomfort in my stomach. Whether this had come from those first beers or from a certain horror as I thought about the circumstance, I felt outside of the real me. I looked back on the evening. Somehow I had ended up in an apartment with a handful of college guys. There were four at the least, but who knows how many were actually preying on us that night? Amy and I were the only girls and this was just beginning to strike me as bad news. Not only were we underage, fifteen to be exact, but also we had nowhere else to go. Somewhere throughout the night our stories ended up twisting into a web of lies to our parents. "We are here; now we're going there," we told them. My stomach coiled tighter as I remembered lying to Dad on the phone. There was no way I could let him know that I had gotten myself into this situation; it was the worst decision I had ever made and I could never look at him the same way if he knew how dumb I had been. No, I decided, I would definitely not be going home that night.

�※

It was yellow.

I use as much concentration as any twelve-year-old has to bend over backwards and look at the basket. The sun, which had put the beads on my forehead, is situated right behind the clear glass and I squint my eyes tighter in order to make the shot. There is no way Dad can make this backwards free throw, and if I can pull it off he will get a "G" and be "PIG." We're tied at our game of "PIG," each with two letters, and the next person who misses a shot made by the other will be the loser. Squinting out the sun, I can see the backboard, the rim, the net, and with my hair falling down my back, I lob the ball over my head and behind me. It actually hits the backboard and circles the rim again and again and aga......in, it's in!!! No way could Dad make that shot, and for the first time after all these years, he is "PIG" and I win with my signature shot. Now, as the loser, it is his job to make us ice waters to revive our bodies from the heat. He hoists me up on his shoulders, putting me four feet closer to the yellow ball in the sky and, just like the sun, I feel on top of the world. I have finally beaten my Dad at "his" game and, although he always tries to win, I know that he is happy for me. He is proud to have a daughter who can beat him in a basketball-shooting contest.

✵

Amy was flirting back as if her life depended on it. Always searching for attention, she was now clearly ecstatic that these older guys were willing to give it. Their attempts at wooing me over were not as successful. I lacked the self-confidence that overflowed in Amy and just couldn't accept the notion that my braces and baby face could remind someone of "Sarah Jessica Parker." That's what he told me! He might as well have just stated that I was the most beautiful girl he had ever seen and that, because he thought so, he should be entitled to get into my pants. I wasn't falling for the cheap lines and I was not ready for the alcohol to get the best of me. Why the hell had I agreed to follow Amy downstairs to "the college guys'" apartment? As I thought back, I didn't even remember agreeing. Did I actually consent to hanging out with these guys, or had I just followed Amy without speaking up? At what point had my 'no' turned to 'yes' when they offered us alcohol? There I was sitting in the apartment of some twenty-year-old horny drunks and I couldn't even remember how the hell I had let myself get into this situation. Emily, what were you thinking? You were only a few seconds away from rape, from violation, from death, for all you knew, when a violent knocking came from the door.

✵

It was red.

As I looked down at the dozen buds, a single tear fell onto one soft red petal. I had received flowers before, but never ones picked out especially by Dad. Although I'm sure he had felt nothing less on any other occasion, his roses made this one special for me. Through this gesture I could feel the pride and happiness he shared in my accomplishments. As I smelled their scent, I pictured Dad watching one of my dance videos by himself simply because he wanted to see it one more time, and I could hear the sound of his voice critiquing pirouettes and leaps like an old pro. I imagine fathers priding themselves in the athletics of their sons and I once again realize that I am all he has. And yet, looking into the twelve open buds that I am sure he thought were overpriced, I know he would want nothing more than to watch me dance one more time and tap the stranger next to him, saying that I was his girl. He was saying something with this act, saying something to his only child about what she meant to him. And during those few seconds when I admired the deep red beauty of the bouquet, I was overcome with an intense gratitude for being the person Dad thought the world of.

If only it had been the police. If only they had come and knocked and taken me home. Then my parents would have yelled at me and hated me, but I'd still have survived. If only I had been the one to suffer the punishment, me and no one else. If only.

If only the T.V. would show the Hawkeye one more time so that I can finish this helmet. I am making Daddy the best Iowa football helmet he's ever seen. I will press hard on the black crayon to make the background as dark as possible; it will be so black, darker than Dad's coffee. The yellow Hawkeye will be outlined perfectly and colored in with a yellow as bright as the sun. When I am finished, I will sign it in rose red: Love, Emily. The red must be the brightest red possible so that everyone will know who made it especially for him.

If only it were someone else, besides Dad, who had knocked at the door.

It will show everyone that the Hawkeyes are Dad's favorite football team.

If only he hadn't seen straight through my lies and called Amy's mom.

It will be so perfect!

If only that twenty-five-year-old drunken bastard hadn't tried to deny the fact that two fifteen-year-old girls were being harbored inside.

Daddy will be able to have his two favorite things right in front of him on his desk, Iowa Hawkeye football and me.

If only I hadn't run straight out of that fucking apartment into my Dad's sight, and if only he had felt no emotion towards that drunken college kid who had been hiding me inside.

Everyone will see it and ask him about it and he will tell them that his only child drew it for him.

If only Dad had just walked over to me instead of pushing him out of the way.

Wasn't she so good at drawing even though she's only eight?

Then maybe I wouldn't be screaming right now.

Yes, she did love football as much as any little boy ever did.

Maybe the bastard wouldn't be chasing after Dad,

She knows all about the yards,

yelling at him and calling him a pussy,

and downs,

swinging him around,

and even safeties.

getting in his face.

She is an Iowa fan, just like me, he'll say,

Dad is telling me to get into the car just as Mr. Sarah Jessica Parker

with a smile on his face and that light in his eye

pulls his right arm back and swings it forward.

that he only gets when he talks about me.

His fist gains more and more speed

Yes, he will love this Hawkeye football helmet.

until it collides with Dad's left eye,

It will be his favoritest thing ever.

and his blood stains the car window next to me.

Well, besides me, that is!

Dad gets in the car and starts driving. He doesn't respond when I ask him if he is all right. He somehow simplifies his emotions into one statement. He expected something like this from Amy, but he could never have expected this from me. He says nothing more. At this point my vision blurs and my heart sinks deep into my stomach. Everything has stopped moving. I don't remember the rest of the drive home, I don't remember walking inside and I don't remember what my mom said or what Dad said to her. All I remember is drinking a glass of cold milk while leaning up against the counter. I keep the glass tilted upwards as to hide my face and keep drinking until it is gone, until there is no more milk and until Dad walks right back out the door and gets in the car to go to the hospital. That last sip of milk slides down my silent throat, past my pained heart, and lies among the queasiness of my stomach, which will remain until Dad's stitches are gone, until his bruise has faded and until I can once again consider myself his daughter, his pride, his favoritest thing ever.

It was deception and cowardice signed in blood.
It was black and yellow signed in red.

I Know That She is Running Somewhere

Matthew Doria

It comes back to me in a slideshow of vivid recollections. The first thing I remember is the panicked sound of my mother's dress shoes racing across the tile floor. It was an unnerving noise; why would my mother be running across the kitchen in her nice shoes?

She ran out the back door and screamed something to me. I know it was something along the lines of "Call the police" or "Get Dad," and I know I understood what she said at the time, but now I cannot remember any words that I heard on that day.

I remember rushing outside, and I remember running to our barn in close pursuit of my mother. Then my blood is turned to ice by a phantom of cold air. I remember seeing my father cry for the first time in my life. I remember the police. I remember the paramedics. I remember my younger sister and her friend crying in her room. I remember my mom's friends coming. I remember my friends coming. I remember crying. And I remember shivering on a humid day in July.

"I can't imagine ever saying good-bye to her for good, so it is just a long sleep I send her off on now. Good night, Emily." That's me, five days later, addressing a gathering of about a thousand people at my older sister's funeral.

So I'm done, but I don't want to leave the pulpit. I don't want to be done. If I'm done, then what do I do next? But I can't just stand here. I have to leave the pulpit. I will leave the pulpit. I will walk away from the altar, which

is decorated with little things to remind us all of her. I will hug my grandmother, then my mother, then my aunt and then my younger sister. I will
listen to the rest of the speakers talk. I will file out of the church and proceed
to the reception, where a woman who taught Home Ec to me will sit me
down and tell me about how my sister will send signs to me from heaven and
that I always have to be looking for them. I will struggle through the next few
weeks in shock. I will board a plane for London, and then I will board a plane
back home. I will say goodbye to my friends as they leave for college, and
then I will leave for college. That's all I have to do.

I leave the pulpit.

If I replay the images that I remember in chronological order, the
cold phantom that overtook my body manifests itself into a vivid scene, and
all of a sudden I am getting out of my car.

I get back from work and I walk across my driveway, up the back
stairs and into the kitchen. I am still exhausted from the night before. After
changing out of my waiter's uniform, I fall asleep in the family room to the
background noise of MTV. At 5:00 my mom tells me that she is worried
about Emily, who has been missing all day. She asks me to go out and check
the barn (at this point I give her a look, which she will later describe as the .
look which made her think the worst). I go out to the barn. There is no sign
of her downstairs, nor do I see her in the loft. I feel a relief come over my
body. I turn the barn light off, never thinking to look in the storage area.

At 7:00, I hear the noise of my mother's dress shoes rushing across
the kitchen floor. She is wielding a pair of scissors, screaming frantically while
racing out to the barn. I call something to my Dad, and then I run after her.
When I get there, she has already cut my sister down. My Dad arrives seconds
later, and there we are, the three of us, standing in the storage area, where we
keep old furniture and unwanted tag-sale items, above my sister. My Dad
recklessly crouches down, trying to somehow revive her.

For some reason I tell my parents that we have to get her outside, as
if the outside air could somehow breathe life into her limp body. My father
and I begin to pick her up when I hear the terrible scream of police sirens.
Her normally light body is so heavy, and her skin is cold and bruised. Her
head hangs over to the right and her neck is dark purple. Her eyes are open,

but they are empty. We try, but even my father and I cannot move her. We rest her down. My father is crying. He is shouting, "Why, Emily?" Or maybe it was "Why *Emily*?"

I cannot stay there. I run away from the scene and collapse against the chimney, which runs up the side of my house next to the driveway. This is where the police and the EMTs find me. They ask me stupid questions and I try to answer, but my tears swallow up my voice. And then it is over.

The next thing I remember, I am in the funeral home, staring down at my sister. My parents, sister Abby and I are allowed to be the first ones in. I stare down at her. I hold her hand. It is still cold, but not in the way it was before. She looks beautiful in her wooden casket, wearing a white dress that reminds me of her prom. Flowers surround her and she looks peaceful, the way the ocean might seem placid once the storm clouds roll over into blue skies. I rub her hair, and then I am eight years old.

"He lives right here," Emily says.

"Wow — right here in our backyard?"

I wasn't creative enough to make my own imaginary friends, so I had to play with hers.

"He's magic, you know. He lives right here in this tree."

"Hello." I rub the tree.

"Don't be stupid. He lives too high up to hear you."

"Oh. Emily?"

"What?"

"How did you find him?"

"He found me."

"Oh. How come he didn't find me?"

"I guess I'm just special."

"She was very special," my mom says between the tears.

"I know, Mom." I hug her.

"No, you aren't," I say.

"Oh yeah? Then why do you think he found me?"

"Because you're bigger."

"She was bigger than life," whispers my mother.

"She lived a lot in twenty years," my father responds in a soothing voice.

"My friend's big, too. He's like twenty years old," Emily says.

"Oh." I look up at the tree. "Does that mean he will die before us?"

"Stop being dumb. Magic people can't ever die."

"Magic people can't ever die," I say.

There is silence.

"Matt, stop."

"What?"

"Stop writing about me."

"Why? What's the matter with what I'm writing?"

"I don't want to be a painful memory."

"What else could I write about?"

"I don't know. I just don't want you to remember me like this."

"You're not a painful memory. You're more. Let me show you."

To get through it, you have to remember the happy stuff. The way she always made people laugh. The way her presence could consume an entire room of people. The way you could be so mad at her, and then she could change everything with only one word. The way she was with children. The way she could make anything fun. The way she never forgot my birthday. The way she never seemed to care what other people thought. The way she told a story. The way she was always the first one up and the last one standing at night.

You feel cheated, mostly. But then sometimes you get this strange sensation. I can't explain it very well, except that it is like the way you might feel if you walked around a corner and an angel accidentally walked right through you. And it hits me. Though Emily's life was haunted by torment, it was still a beautiful thing because I understand, usually for only moments at a time, what beauty really is: "a heart enflamed and a soul enchanted."

The memories are what I hold most dear. I remember her running. It was her favorite thing to do. She was an all-American distance runner in high school, and she trained for long hours every day. I don't know if I believe in heaven, but I do believe that she is running somewhere, and that the pain she felt daily is less than a distant memory.

Maybe that is why running with her is one of the most vivid memories I have, and it reminds me of her in many ways.

We are running beneath majestic trees that sift the sunshine through to us. She is to my left, and the dirt path, cluttered by an occasional root, is passing under me. She is too fast, and I quickly grow tired. I stop. She keeps going. Her back gracefully strides away from me, I picture her growing smaller as she races towards the horizon. A solitary tear plots its own course along her cheek as she runs away. I cannot see it, but it is there. The tear rolls off of her face and plummets toward the path below. It stops for a moment, a foot from the ground, neither it nor its owner yet ready to complete their journey. Then, inevitably, time again turns, and the tear elegantly descends to the awaiting ground. It is absorbed by the dirt as my sister's running form is absorbed by the horizon — a remembrance of a beauty that, for an instant in the eternal chronology of time, graced the world.

Wrong Way Lenny

Marlena Holt

Belligerent, shredding winds buckle tightly around each hearth. The brisk breeze leaves a nip in the air with the potency of over-steeped breakfast tea. In the north: there haunts a beastly storm. Ferocious rain stampedes through the kasha bush and passion fruit vines, and then gnashes its teeth, with acid rain stench, into homes that encase sanguine circles of blood and faith. A bleak downpour torments the nourished abodes into a quaking block. Paradise.

My mother starts to cry. Unpronounced tears emit from her squeezed-shut eyes. One bitter cry-drop falls onto the terra cotta tiles; that one for her Hus-bound, on a rig in Mexico Bay. More come. The second dashes from face to floor in lifelong speed. Her two daughters growing up and growing vastly apart. Three tears, four. Heart beats twice. I never know what to do when a mommy cries.

One hundred and ninety-three minutes have elapsed. Time feels like a traffic jam. Moments of before pound through my head, louder than the volatile rain that pelts our shutters and manages, still, to mist through the screen. Towels drenched. Wet with the storm that seeps into the house like a noxious gas, flooded with the sweat that drips from these Eve-sprung bodies. Imprisoned, and the time passes with moping strokes and brim-full buckets. Every second drips hungrily into a sage, Rubbermaid pail, collecting a puddle of time, hour by hour, day by day.

The eye hits. An unearthly and provocative quiet enshrines the barricaded residents. Yet not a soul emerges. Except my own. Rainwater jackets the kitchen floor and licks at the heels of the raised dining room table. Mother cries again. Duties are known to an accurate daughter. Her eyes lay flat and tell me to find a way. My sister stares at me from behind our mother's trembling shoulders. She seethes acceptance and disdain for what she knows I will do. Acceptance because this is the way it has been and will be: I will obligingly entertain our mother with tasks in which I will persevere until she is happy. Disdain, because I am not selfish enough to permanent marker a line between obedient and enslaved. "Suffer," her silence whispers to me. "Let her suffer and divine in her own daughters' voracity." But instead I am the one to suffer.

Sixteen minutes to finish what I have not begun. I step outside and an immediate shudder overwhelms my heart. A dense charcoal-gray smolders above in the evening sky. The air is barren. Even the deepest breath in feels like an asthmatic drag on a Viceroy. Gripped pickaxe. Moistened gravel. In one swift Ferris-wheel-swoop I heave through the soil. My arms blaze with the intense pressure of time tick-tocking away. My mind dries, brittle and stiff like the rocks I pound farther and farther into with every swing. It's a trench I am trying to create, but to the storm — ferocious, austere — my efforts to advance are as fruitful as those of Sisyphus.

I pick and shovel relentlessly. Each swing with as much moxy as the first. Swings. No longer plastic and chain like those entitled to a childhood. The definitions have changed. I have become a windmill of digging. Every circulating talon retreating from the earth with dirt-dug progression. Muddied clumps infiltrate the space between granite and ground, hovering into free fall before crashing into dust.

Overhead, hurricane sirens begin to whale, their screams flowing around the hills and folding into the valleys. The water comes: a sign that the jumbis ensure curse and disaster. Drops of rain begin to fall: as big as bombs, as hard as nails. A war zone of winds and water. Pulling flower from stem, leaf from tree, and depositing them – kamikaze, A.W.O.L. — into foreign lands with colloquial tongue. There's no place like home.

Lenny leaves. Without a whisper of its existence, Lenny folds into itself until it is nothing more than a hovering spectacle of sand in the turgid, Caribbean sky. No food, more frustration. I venture to "Rosa's Shanty" and pray she is there to receive me in my pursuit to sustain a famished family.

＊

Garbled Cruzan, interlaced with a cacophony of steel pans and heartbeat bass, shrills through the pores of the speakers inside. A deep fryer hisses loudly in the kitchen. Coming closer, I can hear a melodic hymn. It wafts through the air and wanders in and out of ears, tantalizing the mind with snippets of *Lawd Jesus* and *Praise He*. Time freeze. Momentum breeds. I stand, little child, sweetly swaying in the reverence of my *lawd's* compromising embrace. Feed. Family. Provide. Another step closer to my salvation.

"*Eh-eh, chil'! You'! You nah hear? Oooooh, Lawd. 'tis tha melee! Mistah Lenny, dah hurricane ah jus' pass tru here, he ah bock up deh wrong way. Pass meh islan' try, I praise Jesus! But deh jumbis say, 'Hoi' up, Mistah Lenny'! Chuuuuuups! Mistah Lenny ah turn bock aroun' an' head straight to'rds meh home. Meh los' current, an' WAPA won' fix dat nah time soon. But deh Lawd saves. What pah ya here fah?*"

Words walk slowly over my tongue and flatten out as they press through my lips, gaunt and tightly tuned into a rolling pin of white-skinned shame. My "r's" accented out. My "th's" thick with American pronunciation.

"One *roti*," I stammer, "one conch *pate, tr-ee Johnny cake, an' a sal-fish an' funji.*" It finishes with intrinsic vigor. "*Gingah beer.*" My voice demands need, my head demands heart, my heart denies hope.

Steaming soul food rides shotgun home. Deep-fried dough, deep-fried slow-smell-floating from the paper-thin bag of brown. Wandering over said seats of rawhide, underneath mine, overhead me. Wrapping, weaving scent around, odor-bound. Its aroma: permeating through my nostrils, tugging at every hair, tickling every sense. Invading its soul into mine. My eyes begin to burn with the heat of the deep fryer and so I drive until I can see no more. And then I am home.

A black and blue sky delivers to us sugary drops of rain that dance and dive from air to earth to a watery abyss of mud and puddle. Exotically infused bougainvillea blossoms that scream flavor; glistening with the tears from heaven that have fallen for this day, they carpet the land in a pulpy, pink smear of petals. The dripping river washes over me. I am ready. As it drains down to the sea, it takes with it the sins surfaced by the day and swabs the deck of the hurricane plague. Though I can still hear her melodic voice in the air, from up there, she chants, "*Da Lawd saves.*"

AUTHOR'S NOTE: The words written in italic are real. It is a dialect known as Cruzan, which is only a slight variation from English. Cruzan comes from the island of St. Croix, U.S. Virgin Islands, where the story also takes place. Though a majority of the words are simply English ones misspelled, a few words may need explanation for the reader. For example, a *"jumbi"* is an evil or mischievous spirit, and the word *"current"* is Cruzan for electricity.

"Measure Your Life in Love"*

Christine Mitchell

How do you measure the life of a woman or a man?
You measure in...

That Tuesday, I walked out of my theatre class, through the quad, and saw a familiar face. It was Peter. With a big smile, as usual, on his face, he waved to me. As I walked over to him, I thought about how it's only September 11th, and I already feel like I have some good friends. Peter and I greeted each other casually and were talking about our classes that had just finished. I bragged that I had arranged my schedule so I only had one class for the day, and that now it was over.

As we chatted, one of Peter's old buddies from high school walked over. Marc said to us, "Can you guys believe this?" Peter and I both looked at him as if he were crazy. Marc said, "A plane, a terrorist hit the World Trade Center!" Our eyes lit up. I assumed he was just joking with us. Peter was quiet. I immediately questioned, "Wait, the Twin Towers are the World Trade Center, right?" I had never referred to the Twin Towers as the World Trade Center. Marc affirmed it. And I thought, "Oh my God, I was just there!"

In midnights?

I met Kristin, Matt and Christine on the ferry at about 9:00 PM. "This is probably my last trip into Manhattan for a while," I thought. As usual with them, we joked and kidded during the entire ferry ride. Once we arrived in Manhattan, we took the subway up to Times Square, where we figured we could get something to eat. When entering the restaurant, Kristin and I sneaked off and told the waiter that it was Matt's birthday. We chose Matt because he is quiet, and we knew he would get embarrassed easily. After we ate, the whole restaurant began to sing as the staff brought over a cake. Matt was completely mortified. He retaliated by smearing his cake all over our faces.

After dinner, it was already midnight. We must have been in the restaurant forever, I thought. I was beginning to get nervous about being home for my 1:00 AM curfew. I decided that we would take another subway line back in order to be closer to the ferry terminal. By the time the subway came, I realized there was no way I would be home by one; the next boat was not until 12:30 and that would only get me to Staten Island by one, after which I would have to drive a half an hour to my house. I called my parents and told them I was taking the 12:30 boat. When we approached the Canal St. subway stop, the conductor announced that this was the last stop because of construction. I panicked. It was 12:15; we had to get onto the 12:30 boat, or my parents would kill me. We had to travel by foot from Canal St. to the ferry terminal in fifteen minutes. If you know New York, you know what a long distance this is, so I made everyone run.

We started running and Kristin said, out of breath, that she MUST stop to go to the bathroom. So, we approached the Twin Towers, and we went in so that she could use the bathroom. Into the basement we went, running completely out of breath. The basement was huge; we were in the level of the mall. Just picture four of us, three girls in skirts and a boy, running through this mall at 12:20, rummaging, looking desperately for a bathroom. Eventually, we found one, Kristin and Christine went in and I waited outside with Matt. Now, I was completely freaking out about my parents. When Kristin and Christine came out, I made it clear that we had to get to the ferry terminal in less than ten minutes, so we HAD to haul it. Matt took the lead and we started running to get out of the Twin Towers. We got completely lost down there; we could not find an exit to the street anywhere. Eventually, we got out of the Towers, and we jetted down Broadway to the ferry terminal. I was screaming the whole way for us to run faster. And, believe it or not, we just made the ferry. On the boat, we were completely covered in sweat and dying because of the heat.

We actually had a ton of fun that night, and this was my last memory I have with my friends because I came up to Boston the next afternoon.

I still was a little skeptical about believing Marc's claim that the Twin Towers were hit by a plane. Therefore, Peter and I walked into a building and merged with a crowd of people whose eyes were glued to two television sets. We saw it. We both looked up and saw the landmark building of our city up in flames. Peter and I just looked at each other in complete and utter shock. Tears streamed down our faces. The Twin Towers are Manhattan. They make the city. "This was my home," I thought. I have driven by the skyline of the city so many times and stared at the Twin Towers, just marveling at them.

A couple of minutes passed, and I thought of my friend, Maureen, from back home, whose father worked in the Towers. I became worried, so I decided to go back to my room and start making some phone calls. I left Peter and headed for the bus stop. As I was walking through the quad, I thought, what about Erica's dad? His law firm is just outside the Towers. Next, I thought of Kristin's dad, who is a firefighter stationed in Times Square. It wasn't until I saw my friend, Joe, who is from the Bronx, that I mentioned my dad. I looked at him and said, "Oh my God. My dad is a fireman in Manhattan. I hope he's okay." Then I started to run to the bus stop to go back to my dorm to call home.

On the bus, everyone was talking about my city. I also heard rumors: the White House was on fire, the Pentagon was hit, Camp David was hit and there were still more hijacked planes in the air. Everyone was offering his or her commentary on the attacks, but all I could do was pray that my dad was not working today.

When I got off the bus in Newton, I ran to my dorm. I could not think of anything except calling home. I picked up the phone, and I tried to dial home, but I got a strange, fast busy signal. After trying numerous times to call both home and my sister's house in Boston, I gave up with the phone. I then turned on the television and sat down, glued to it. It was unreal to watch. Both Towers had now collapsed. What was I watching? This could not be real. They continually showed reruns of the second plane hitting the second tower, and then the Towers collapsing shortly afterwards. Then, the announcer casually mentioned, "All New York City Firefighters were called back in to work on this fire." My heart skipped a beat. I know my dad, and I know he definitely went to help. He would never miss this "excitement," as he would call it. He lived for fires like this. I knew that he would be talking about it for years to come.

A couple of hours had passed by, and I attended Mass outside at school. When I came home, my grandmother was on my voice mail, saying that my dad was working at 15th Street in Manhattan, but he was relieved early, about a half-hour before the fires. He was not home yet, which was understandable because, knowing him, he definitely went back to the fire when he heard about it. It was about 3:00, and I still did not hear anything about my dad. I began to get a little upset. By now, almost everyone on my floor knew about my dad being there. I needed someone at this point, so I went down to Peter's room. Peter and I sat in his friend Pat's room (Pat was from Queens), and we were there for a couple hours on the couch, just glued to the television. Pat was starting to get very upset. No one from his family was there, but he just loves New York. In his room, he even has a massive poster of the city skyline. It was depressing to just sit there, watching the reports, most of which ended up being false. I had to do something.

I went back upstairs to my room, and I attempted to call home. I could not get through. I tried my sister in Boston, and I got through. She had no idea about our dad, so I had to tell her. She became upset and said that I should come over and stay with her. I went.

When I arrived there, she had cooked dinner for us. After dinner, we needed a distraction, so we walked over to her friend Dan's house, even though I was starting to get nervous and upset. I did not want to show this to my sister, though. I am always the tough one in our family, and if I am crying, she gets worried. All I really wanted to do now was to go back to my room, be alone and call my old volleyball coach, Mr. Mahon, and cry to him.

In times that we cried?

I came home directly from high school, probably the first time all year. I was always staying after to do some sort of extra-curricular activity. But not today. I was so tired I could hardly move. There was a volleyball club going on that day, but I skipped it and came home. I took the train and then walked to my house. I walked in and greeted my father. I told him about how tired I was and how I was going to sleep very shortly. I told him about my day at school. When I told him how I received an 80 on my political science midterm, which was a good grade for that class, he flipped out. He thought that I was not doing enough schoolwork, that I was slacking off. I never slack off. I am very determined. "I am actually really happy with that grade," I said. My dad laughed. He said, "Do you care about your marks at all? You need your average to be high for the first term because they get sent to colleges on your mid-year school reports," he said. At this point, I had enough, "Dad, I am trying my hardest. I was happy with that grade. I have heard enough about the stupid mid-year school reports. I get it," I yelled. He just kept saying, "You are not going to get into a good school if you do not keep your marks up. This is so important. You worked so hard all through high school, don't blow it now." This upset me so much because I was trying my best. I ran in my room, lay down on my bed, started crying and could not stop. It was not just this incident that upset me. With my dad, I always felt like I had to be perfect. I felt this constant pressure to always be the best. I could not take it anymore.

My dad left for work shortly after, and I could not sit in my room any more. I left my house, and drove back to school. I knew Mr. Mahon would be there because of volleyball club. I walked into the gym, went over to him and started crying about the fight with my dad. Mr. Mahon and I had already been very close; he was my coach for four years and a teacher at my school. He was extremely nice to me, and he cheered me up over the course of the practice. Mr. Mahon made me realize that my dad really did mean well. He loved me more than anything, and he just wanted me to do well and succeed. My dad always wanted the best for me, but sometimes, he just did not express it correctly.

I tried to argue with my sister that I felt awkward sitting at her friend's house (a friend I did not even know). I offered to go alone back to my dorm, and I said that I would just meet her back there later. This did not work. She ended up getting really annoyed and started yelling at me. My sister is also like my dad in that you can never win an argument against either of them. There is really no use in trying. I needed to cry to someone, though. I wanted to see Peter and cry to him if I could not call Mr. Mahon. I needed someone, but I could not convince my sister.

We went to her house again later, and she decided that I should sleep there that night. In the morning, when I woke up, I had the urge to go back home to New York. My father had not called home since Monday night, and I had the feeling this was not that good, even though I tried to convince my sister that it was not bad yet.

When we called our mom that morning, she said she made arrangements for us to come home, which all of us wanted. I took the trolley and the BC Bus back to my dorm, grabbed some clothes and necessary items, ran back to get the BC Bus and then took the trolley back to Jen's house. Someone picked us up there shortly thereafter, and we were on our way home. When we were driving through Brooklyn, I could not take my eyes off of the skyline. It was non-existent. It did not look like New York City. It could have been Boston, Chicago or even Jersey City, for all I knew. "That is not New York," I thought, for I could not believe my eyes. It is amazing what evil people are capable of.

When I arrived at my home on Staten Island, it was a solemn place. My mother and grandmother were outside, awaiting our arrival. My mother warned me to go directly upstairs, because many of my family's friends were downstairs. I was so hungry. Someone had brought bagels over. I saw them and immediately grabbed one. (Bagels were my favorite thing in the world: New York Bagels only, though.) I was glad to be with my mom and grandmother. The four of us and my dad were the only family members that I ever talked to. It was good we were all together.

On Thursday, a group of firefighters came to our house. They were all friends of my father. One of them vacations with us every summer, so I feel I know him very well. The other guys I hardly even knew, but they were funny. All we were doing was telling stories about my dad. Before my dad was promoted, he was a firefighter in a company in Brooklyn for fifteen years. That company was always his home. These guys knew my father very well. They were telling a recent story about my father that really made me laugh. There was a new guy at the firehouse who was very heavy. He had gained a ton of weight over the six months that he was on the job. My dad, who was no longer in this firehouse, used to abuse this guy. Any day that the guy was working, my dad would get there early on his way to work in Manhattan and make this guy go running with him or do pushups with him. My dad was determined to get this guy in shape. This reminded me of when my dad used to force me to go running. I absolutely hated running, but my dad would want me to go running with him, and he would pester me until I finally gave in and went. I absolutely hated running.

After the firemen left, more people came inside. The days seemed to go by very quickly because so many people were constantly in and out of my house. The phone never stopped ringing. So many people brought us food. By Friday night, we had five trays of lasagna, three trays of chicken cutlets and every imaginable type of dessert. As the days went on, my hope and faith that my dad would come home slowly dwindled down. A week after the incident, I spoke with my old friend from high school, John. I had not spoken to

John in about a year and a half. My mom always said, "Tragedies like this bring out the best in people, and it really makes people come together."

In bridges we burned?

John was my best friend for about two years: my sophomore and junior years in high school. He was the greatest and nicest guy. He was a year older than I was, and when I was a junior, we went to the prom together. Riding in our limo to the prom was a girl I did not get along with at all. She was John's best friend's date. At the prom, this girl was all over John. I was so annoyed with her, but John did not stop her either, which annoyed me even more.

Most of my friends were at the prom that year, so I went and cried with them in the bathroom. It was an ugly scene. Even worse, John did not even know I was mad at him. He was clueless. By the ride home, though, he knew. He was scared about how mad I was. He said, at one point, "You're not going to be mad at me for a while after this, right?" I intended to be mad at him for a long while. That was the worst thing he could have possibly done to me because it made this girl so happy to break us apart. It was exactly what she wanted.

For the next week, he called me several times, but I would not talk to him. A week later, we were at the same athletic awards dinner. I tried to avoid him all night, and I succeeded until the end of the dinner. I did not want to make a scene because his parents were there. I was sitting alone at my table with my friend, Christine, when John sat down next to me. He stared at me, but I did not even want to look at him. He apologized, and we eventually made up. Two days later was the last day of school. I saw him then, and I gave him a kiss and a hug. This was the last time that I spoke with him. It was weird because we both just did not call each other all summer, and he went away to school in August.

When I spoke with John, it was very comforting. It was as if we had not missed any time together.

That night, my dad's firehouse in Brooklyn was having a get together for the missing firemen and their families. There were seven firefighters missing from that house. The firemen said something to us that night which just seems to stick out in my memory: "The firehouse is your house. If you need anything, let us know." At the party, we pieced together the details of where exactly my dad had been on September 11th.

In truths that emerge?

My Dad was relieved a half-hour early from work, which was twenty minutes before the Trade Center was hit. He had the radio on in his car (when we picked up his car, the radio was blaring on an all-news station) and he heard about all firemen being called in to work. He went to his old firehouse in Brooklyn, parked his car, grabbed someone's jacket and helmet from inside, got in a car with a chief and another lieutenant, and went to the Trade Center. (Both the Chief and the Lieutenant have been assumed dead.) Because he was not on duty, he was not initially allowed into the fires. He was talking with someone outside the command center when the first tower went down. They both ran, but after getting away safely, my dad went back, unlike the man he was with. Someone saw him requesting a flashlight, and someone else saw him "running down the street with his jacket open, his helmet on, flashlight in hand and he ran right into Tower One, which was still standing."

Or the way that you died?

Friday morning, my sister and I came back up to Boston. My mother did not want us to miss any more school. She was concerned about our grades. My dad also would want us to be back in school. He would want us to continue on. He valued our education so much. He wanted more than anything for my sister and me to succeed in life. He always pushed us to do and be our best in school and in athletics. Anything less than giving our best was not acceptable to him. He made me become as ambitious, as moral and as persistent as I am today. Whatever I do with my life, I know it will be because of him. He worked two jobs in order to be able to afford to send my sister and me to a great school like Boston College. He loved my sister and me more than anything. For the rest of my life, I will live in the morals that my father has instilled in me. I will do everything that I can to continue to make him proud.

* Lyrics are taken from the song, "Seasons of Love," from the Broadway musical, *Rent*, composed by Jonathan Larson, 1996."

Reflection *and* Meditation

The Uncertainty

Chiazor Okagbue

Turning and turning in the widening gyre
The falcon cannot hear the falconer;
Things fall apart; the center cannot hold;
Mere anarchy is loosed upon the world,
The blood-dimmed tide is loosed, and everywhere
The ceremony of innocence is drowned.

—an excerpt from W.B. Yeats' "The Second Coming"

The rocky gray path begins to look smooth under my sneakers as I increase my pace. The heavy backpack is weighing me down, but I push forward. My dorm seems farther away than usual. Rounding the corner, I spot the square plot of gravel that is the makeshift parking lot for the dorms on the north side of campus; there is no sign of my mother's car. *Where could they possibly be?* As I wave my identification card in front of the black sensor at the entrance of my dorm, I hear someone yell my name. "Chiazor!" I turn in the direction of the cement athletic center. Parked in front of the gym is my mother's small black car and standing in front of her car are my uncle and aunt. I throw off the bulky backpack and dash towards them.

I curl myself into a tight fetal position on the wide green futon. My arms hold my knees close to my chest until I think I'm going to explode from the increasing pressure. As I rest my head on the hard white wall, the hand of darkness in the cube-shaped room creeps closer to me. With every slow, deep breath, I can feel the invisible fingers creeping their way

59

over the goose bumps on my trembling body. Someone help me. I stare at the wild pink and green patterns on the faded Oriental rug lying motionless on the black linoleum floor. My eyes dart to the wrinkled picture on my dresser. The old woman in black and white stares back, a blank look on her face. Why do I have to die, too? But there is no answer. God, are You there?

In my uncle's thin arms I can smell the fruits, spices and soups I have missed in the eight years I have been away from Nigeria. I look up at his face and notice the thick, wide-framed glasses covering the light brown eyes. His skin is rough and much darker now. He also has a wealth of gray hair. I cannot remember him being this old, but of course it has been so long. His colorful blue and green traditional garb sends me back to the moment he held my nine-year-old frame before my mother and I boarded the plane after our last visit. My aunt comes over and runs her thick fingers through my hair. She has not changed so much. The long Nigerian gown she is wearing stops at her ankles, revealing sleek brown sandals. "You've gotten so big and look at how long you hair is," she says with a sigh.

The small photograph rests on a white background within a square black frame. The picture is a fading black-and-white of my grandmother in her earlier years. Her hair is parted on one side and held back with a few pins. She has a slight smile, showing how calm she felt on that particular day. This is a passport size photograph, so you can only see from her chest up. The sleeves of the boat neck sundress she is wearing are scattered with white palm trees in a random design. A large white beaded necklace hangs heavily on her neck, stopping just between her breasts. Her small ears are adorned with matching beaded earrings. The smooth wrinkleless face stares out into space.

My cube-shaped room is dimly lit by the small lamp resting on my desk. I hunch over and open my chemistry textbook. There is nothing I hate more than balancing equations. I have been rubbing my forehead over the same question for the past ten minutes. My phone rings. I glance up at the alarm clock on the shelf. It is almost nine o'clock, so I know it is my mom. She is the only person who ever calls this early. I let the phone ring a few more times before picking up the cordless receiver. "Hi, Mom," I mutter with some exasperation.

"How did you know it was me?" she asks jokingly.

"I hate these stupid chemistry equations," I whine.

"I would let your uncle help you, but he's not feeling so well. I think he might have food poisoning. He got really sick after we ate dinner and his stomach still hurts."

"Well, tell him I hope he feels better."

"I'm taking him to the hospital tomorrow."

"Okay, then. I better go if I'm going to get any sleep tonight."

"Love you."

I shrug off the phone call and continue to pick away at the chemistry problem.

❁

My grandmother and I share a deeply spiritual bond. Reincarnation is mysterious. The idea that someone else is alive within me thrills yet scares me. My grandmother died of a stroke one month before I was born. My family believes that on September 6, 1983, when I came into this world, she came back to them. I have always been known as "Mommy" to my mother, aunts and uncles. The thick red lips, full head of wiry hair, anxious eyes, listening ears and electrifying energy. How can I not be her? My grandmother is me and I am her, but she is dead and I am alive.

❁

The brown flecks sprinkled on the white tiled floor look like dirt against my white sneakers. The walls of the endless hallway are painted light rose and decorated with several framed paintings by famous artists. The smells of medicine, chemicals, machinery and sickness mix together and contaminate the air. An elderly Asian woman is wheeled into the hallway on a stretcher. Her puffy and ashen face is the only visible part of her body. Her head is thickly wrapped with a bandage and her body, from the neck down, is covered with a thin white blanket — her early grave. I gasp at her mummified appearance and pinch the sleeve of my mother's blouse. She looks at me and forces a smile. The stress of the past two weeks has given her puffy eyes, more wrinkles and an unbelievable amount of gray hair.

"Here it is," I hear my uncle say softly. "The Radiology Department." He had been walking down the treacherous hall ahead of us. We women — my aunt, my mother and I — shuffle slowly behind him as if we were following a casket in a funeral procession. Before entering the small waiting room, I catch a glimpse of Monet's *Water Lilies* by the entrance. *If only this were a picture of our lives right now.* The doctor had "felt something" in my uncle's stomach and now they have to do a CT scan to see what it is. We know the diagnosis will determine the treatment needed to make my uncle better, but we already know what is wrong. No one wants to say it, but the truth hangs at the edge of our brains, stealing our sleep, our appetites and our happiness, when we should be enjoying a quiet Christmas together.

I look again into the eyes of this beautiful woman who I supposedly am. I cock my head to one side of the wall, still staring. Her eyes are dark and deep. They can see through me and read my thoughts. I feel them burning a hole in my body and searching my soul. Answer me, Grandma. Help me deal with this. I hope that if I look long enough, a light will shine from the ceiling or an arm might reach out from the small picture. She will know what I can do because she is me in the next life. We are two but we are also one. My grandmother was the last to die and with her went the center of the family. I am the new center, but I cannot hold myself together. Things continue to fall apart.

The phone rings. It is only five o'clock. I scrunch up my face, puzzled as to why someone would be calling so early. I close the "Solitaire" window on my computer screen and pick up the receiver.

"Hi, Mommy," my mom's cheerful voice says. What a relief. She has not been so happy in the past few days.

"Hi. How's everything?"

"Good. Your uncle is doing better." This is great news because we did not know what to expect from the treatment he had received.

"When can I come home and visit him?"

"Soon." There is slight hesitation in the way she says that. "You know you have to keep up with your school work."

"Whatever. I can always catch up if I miss one day. Can I talk to him now?"

"Oh, not right now," she says with a deep sigh. This is a sign of more hesitation. I begin to wonder what my mom is trying to hide from me.

"Okay, Mom — what is it that you're not telling me?" Being in boarding school has its limitations. Not coming home from school everyday has made me a stranger to our family's inner circle. My mom, aunts and uncles have erected walls that I am unable to penetrate, leaving me in the dark.

"Well, your uncle was given some muscle relaxants last night because he was very restless. The problem is that he has been in a coma since this morning."

"Is it that bad?" I ask, knowing that it is. My head seems to spin and I cannot focus on any of the objects around me.

"We're just waiting to see if he will come out of it completely. He keeps mumbling, so we know that he is somewhat conscious."

I cannot say anything after this. There is so much going on that my thoughts are not clear.

"Let me put the phone to his mouth and see if he can recognize your voice. Hold on."

I do hold on. I grip the receiver as if it were the last lifeline I have. The longer I hold on, the weaker my body becomes. There is no sound on the other end of the line. I can hear some static, probably the rustling of bed sheets.

"Say hi to Chiazor."

I can hear my mother's fading voice from a growing distance. I focus on my grandmother's face resting on my dresser, but the silence just hangs.

❋

The living room is dark when I step in. Despite the sun shining outside, all of the curtains and blinds are pulled shut. My aunt is sprawled on the sofa in a blue sweat suit. Her hair is hidden under a scarf, but the scarf is tied on crookedly so I can see tufts of stringy unbrushed hair. She is on the phone with someone, so I sit on the arm of the cream leather sofa instead of running to her. Her voice is soft and her speech slow. When she finally ends the conversation, I rush into her arms. "I missed you, Aunty," my muffled voice says as she squeezes my head into her chest. I try to lift myself up, but she continues to hold me close to her. I can hear her sobbing now. My eyes dart around in the confusion. My mom comes down the stairs and pulls me away from my aunt's strong grasp.

"What's wrong with her?" I ask, still puzzled. My mom puts her arm around me and gazes directly into my eyes. Even though she does not look distressed, I can feel that something is wrong. "When are we going to the hospital?" That is, after all, the purpose of my visit. My uncle had finally woken up from his coma, so my mom brought me home to see him.

"We can't go to the hospital," my mom says, looking down at the ring on her finger.

"Why not? That's why I'm here, isn't it?"

"I don't know how else to tell you this." She pauses to let out a soft sigh. "Uncle Vince died." The last part of that sentence rings loudly in my ears. "Uncle Vince died." What does she mean? How can he possibly be dead if I am home to see him?

"But, Mom, you told me he was better." My voice is beginning to croak.

"I know...I know. He really did wake up on Tuesday night, but then Wednesday morning the hospital called to say that he had stopped breathing."

"Wednesday? Today is *Saturday.*" More walls. "But...But...I didn't say goodbye." The anger begins to rise with my tone of voice.

"None of us did. He died in his sleep." My mom attempts to make eye contact, but I look away, disgusted with her betrayal.

"NO! You've all been here with him the whole time. I'm the only one who didn't even get a chance to look at him. To touch him." I run up the stairs to my room. I fall into the pink beanbag next to my window. The rays of sunlight penetrating through the blinds create streaks of light on my khaki pants. Tears burn my cheeks, falling onto the light rays and making them dark. I do not even bother to wipe them away. There is no point in holding back my emotions. In my excitement, I did not even take off my jacket. Now I want to go back to school, far away from the misery hanging in our gloomy home. I look around my room, hoping to see my grandmother's small face smiling into the space that is time between the two of us. Instead, I see nothing. She is not here. Then maybe I should not be here, either.

As selfish as it sounds, I do not cry for my uncle. I cry for myself. The evil truth of life has been revealed to me in the darkest of ways. I have always known that people eventually die, but my carefree attitude did not allow me to place myself in that category. Now that my uncle is lost to me forever, a part of me is lost, too. He brought some of Nigeria back to me through his visit. The country of my origin has been a mystery for most of my life because only four of my seventeen years were spent living there. Now I am beginning to fade away, piece by piece. My dying process has begun.

The room becomes darker. I can no longer see my grandmother's face on the dresser. The pink and green colors of the Oriental rug have blended in with the shadows around me. I squeeze my eyes shut, afraid that an unwelcome visitor might appear. This paranoia eats away at my confidence, self-esteem and power. It tortures me with every blink and every breath, but I continue to give in to it, a prisoner in my own white-walled cube.

Scarred

Thomas R. Forsythe

I can't imagine missing a set of my scars. They are reminders of the pain that made me. They were born from the hurt that taught me to be who I am. They are a part of me.

Fat instilled in me a fire. I know the burn of discrimination: the obese are a minority. Prejudice lit me aflame and I tend to the fire daily. Injustice has no place in *my* world. I live for fair play, and my fat taught me to be a referee.

"You're fat because you don't like pain!" Did my gym teacher actually just say that to me? Who does he think he is? He does not know me: the real me. He knows a fat kid who is awkward on a tennis court and hates running track. I am a person beneath this flesh. But what can I do to this man? He has control of my life every other day for forty minutes. I dread it, but it is inevitable: by law, even the fat kids have to go to gym class.

"You eat too much! You can't finish your project. Sit down!" Again? My art teacher won't let me finish my papier-mâché turtle because I'm fat. I fail to see the logic. I fail to see anything but red. Once more, though, he is a teacher, so he has intermittent control over me. What can I do?

"He said the same thing to me, Tom."

"He said I was a cow."

"He called me fat, too, but he decides our grades. Let it go."

Never again. I let this happen once; it will *not* happen again.

"I have a problem with a teacher. He told me I ate too much and he wouldn't let me do my work. My friends have had the same problem, but they are scared." The principal nods slowly and flashes a falsely reassuring smile.

He agrees to "talk to" my art teacher, and then later tells me that he has "taken care of the problem." Nothing changes. My art teacher is not disciplined for his ignorance. It is allowed to fester in his skull, even though he teaches children. He helps them create art, but he destroys their self-worth.

I refused to be one of them, though. This was a spark of inspiration of who I am today. I accepted it and was engulfed in the flames of who I now am. My fat gave me a voice because the hell it bound me to gave me fire.

I was first scarred years before, on a lazy summer afternoon. Waves of heat rose off of the pavement as friends from the neighborhood played in my yard. Me: I was enjoying a Snickers bar. I always thought of candy as a treat, and this was apparently a problem. One of the kids in the yard shouted, "No wonder you're fat; you eat candy bars!" My reaction was an honest one (I had not yet built up anything in the way of a defense): "Fat people have to eat, too, ya know!" Slowly but surely, from that day forward, my eating disappeared from view. Even today, the lighter me wants to hide his food until he is alone to eat in private.

Now, I am in a totally new environment, and surrounded by complete strangers. Here, I am only allowed to eat food in a public atmosphere, in front of people I've just met. Welcome to college, please check your emotional baggage at the state line.

"You're coming out to eat with us tomorrow night, right, Tom?" My roommate's mom invites me to dinner. My parents hadn't come to visit this weekend like everyone else's had. I was okay with that — I didn't need to see them again so soon — but I was bored. Everyone else was out shopping or eating with their parents, so there were very few orphans left behind in the dorm. *It was nice of her; she doesn't know she's prodding one of my scars.* I can't eat in front of them, that's all there is to it. But how can I tell them this without being rude? They know the food in the dining hall is bad, and they know that is where I will eat. They know that I am here alone until all of the little freshmen begin to return home. In their minds, I must prefer being a hermit to having *their* company — it is the only explanation.

"We'll see how things look...."

I can't do it!

The next day: "Are you sure you don't want to come?"

"Yeah, I have a lot of work to do."

You are supposed to learn at college. Who knew I would be learning to feel comfortable eating in public? College is changing me, though not overnight. It is a process, as learning always is. Still, it is forming a unique salve for my emotional burns. It hurts, and it's uncomfortable to wear day after day, but my scars are fading.

A dietician's visit to my Home and Careers class in seventh grade cautioned me about scars I had yet to bear, before I was ready to grasp them. During her discussion, she mentioned that people with eating disorders don't see themselves properly. She depicted them in front of a mirror being asked to show how wide they were with their hands. A person with an eating disorder might spread his or her arms as far apart as they would go, even if ribs jutted out from beneath the skin. This idea amazed me. No twelve-year-old can imagine such a concept. I thought, "Wow, these people have eating disorders because of problems with their eyes? That is truly amazing!" I never thought that would be me — until I lost weight. To this day, I still can't use a mirror properly. My vision is fine. It's my mind that doesn't want to see my true self.

My fat skewed my sense of reality. This might be because I have never stopped thinking I was fat. I cannot type, "I am not fat anymore" without flinching. I think, "But I am still fat, people are going to think I don't realize this." Denial, when an actual problem existed, caused this. I know my friends were just trying to spare my feelings by denying the existence of my fat. It was thoughtful, but how am I supposed to trust anyone telling me I am not fat now: after years of them lying to my plump face?

As my fat slowly left me, scar tissue replaced it. My eyes are trained to look in the mirror and see fat. I stretch my arms as far as they go, but scars hide my ribs from view. I will never know if I am fat or not.

The funny thing about a scar: it means you are healed, but it never lets you forget why it is there. The injury stays with you. You can't feel the pain anymore, but you are forever changed by it. My scars do not disfigure me — they decorate me.

The One-Eyed Man

Mason Cole

Y ou can't escape who your ancestors were. When we talk about someone's
looks, we connect him or her with his or her parents. ("He has his father's
nose." "She has her mother's eyes.") Our first source of information about
the world is our family, and later their approval or disapproval plays a role in
determining our adult makeup. My Native American ancestors took this concept even further — they believed that your ancestors would always influence
you in some way, even from beyond the grave.

It sounds wonderful, this tying together of generations with an
unseverable cord. I used to love Indian philosophy for that reason. On long
runs, I would imagine all of my ancestors with me, their spirits sustaining
mine even as my body flagged. It was a comfort to know that when other
children abandoned me at school for reading too much or being too smart,
there was a group of people (long gone, but people, nonetheless) who stood
by me because I had parts of them inside me. Their spirits were a comfort.

But I've turned away from this philosophy in recent years. Every
sword, you see, has a second edge. The blade that cut your bonds today might
have its razor-sharp sights on you tomorrow. I spent much of my life bliss-
fully unaware that the point of a dagger lay just behind my head. This dagger,
of course, wasn't an actual blade; it was simply a metaphor for a man inside
the veterans' medical care facility in Norman, Oklahoma. Some of my worst
memories involve that brick building and the horror inside its walls.

The spotless and sterile corridors were always the same, tiled and
official. Antiseptic smell filled the air, that nasty odor of stagnation. I was
with someone else on these rare trips — either my father or my grandmother,
often both. We took the same route through the building each time, past the

disabled corridors to the mental ward. I always shivered while walking through those doors, even on hot summer days. I was moving into a world where everyone was blind in the worst way — they could still see, but could not make sense of what they saw anymore.

These men all had Alzheimer's disease. Their condition because of it was pathetic. I know. I've experienced it, or imagined that I have.

I've always had a peculiar sense of empathy with those in pain, and I suffer while watching people suffer — always sharing their fate. Walking through those hallways, unable to suppress my empathy, was the equivalent of performing a lobotomy on myself. I fought to maintain indifference, clinical detachment (though I didn't always know the term for it, I knew damn well what it was, and I wanted it) and a sense of perspective — to keep even one mental eye intact in this sightless land.

Resolution always gave way to reality, though. While walking down the hall, my mind leaped from person to person. I sat in a wheelchair looking blankly at a wall, and then found myself slowly walking past my parents and me — moving back down the hall on a journey to nowhere. I talked in nonsense words to friends long dead, and thought I understood what I was saying. I watched cartoons and smiled blankly. By the time we had reached my grandfather's room, I was never sure whether I was a visitor or a patient. And then there was the moment I dreaded most of all. I had to visit this ancestor of mine.

I sat quietly while my grandmother or father would walk up to his bedside and hold his hand, repeating the same phrase over and over. "John, I'm here, John. It's me." A child's phrase, said to reach a child's mind. No — that's a suspect analogy. Children get smarter. They learn to walk and talk and use the toilet instead of fouling their pants early in their lives. My grandfather was doing the opposite, heading the wrong way on what a compassionate God would mark down as a one-way street. Childhood is about building your identity, the very thing that was slipping from my grandfather's grasp.

After a short time, the words being spoken out loud and the thoughts running around in my head would tangle so much that I couldn't tell what I thought and what I heard. I watched as my grandmother would hold up her wedding ring in front of his face. It's a pretty ring, I thought to myself. And, John, it's our sacred bond, and I'm never taking it off. I listened as my father talked about the Oklahoma University football team. The Sooners have always been my favorite, I thought. And, gosh, they're doing great again, Dad;

you'd love to see them playing like they used to. Talk to me, John, Dad, Pop-pop. Let me know you're there.

I wished for a book on every trip to the room. I read the instructions on the bed; I read the warning labels on the medical equipment. I tried to ground myself in the comforting reality of words. I knew that if I looked directly into his eyes, I would begin to imagine myself in his place, just as I always did with the other patients in the corridor. Looking up from that bed and seeing my grandmother and father — and myself — crowded around me would have been a waking nightmare. It was a resolution I managed to keep.

After a while, when my grandmother and father had received a faint spark of recognition (or what passed for one), they would tell me about their cherished memories of the mentally dear departed who left his living body behind. Mason, you should have been there on our wedding day. He made such a handsome figure. Oh, look at him, he's still moving his feet to the music playing on the radio; he was a marvelous dancer. When I was your age, Son, my father took me to Oklahoma football games like the one we're going to today. He once bought us scalped tickets on the day of the game, not a cheap proposition, so I could see the Sooners play Nebraska. And to serve his country in the Air Force for a quarter century, fixing planes with his natural mechanical genius...what a man. A better husband there never was. A better father never lived.

It made me nauseous. I never doubted the truth of their memories, but still I knew that they were living in a fantasy world. The only things they remembered about this man were those that made him out to be a hero, the easiest kind of selective memory to have. At his bedside, he was the only diapered king in the world. Even the first time I went to visit him, I knew that you couldn't speak poorly of Pop-pop while he was in the room. It was one of the few subjects absolutely forbidden to discuss there.

But outside the room, I heard other stories. My grandfather may have been all they said, but he was much more. Isn't everybody? He had been an alcoholic, and although I can't remember ever hearing about him beating my father, my uncle or my grandmother, there were times when such a thing was darkly hinted at. He wasn't a brilliant man — he started out several grades ahead of my grandmother in school, but they graduated in the same class, nevertheless. He attended the local Methodist church and was a member, but never let anyone know his beliefs in matters of faith.

From hearing my relatives talk in that small room, my grandfather made the sun and planets move across the sky. Listening to stories about his faults and shortcomings made him feel real...almost human. It was a feeling I desperately wanted. It kept the nightmares away.

I was never able to accept the fact that the broken shell I was looking at on those hospital visits was a man. Whatever makes up a person's humanity had left him. And every time I visited, though he seemed in his most lucid moments to recognize everyone else in the room, he couldn't spare a spark of recognition for me. My father and grandmother always told me, at these times, stories about the two of us together. Apparently this tough Air Force sergeant, this muscular man with a capacity for words that several years later would get my mouth a good soap-washing, was tender with me. He loved to play with me, he loved to buy me presents, and he loved to watch me ride around the pavement near his house on my tricycle, one of the aforementioned presents. These things I have been told and they are sacred writ. Glory be to John, amen.

I must be told about him, you see. I have only one memory of him, so dim and shot through with static that I can't even be sure of its reality. It involves that same tricycle, that same pavement, that same grandfather. It also involves my tricycle horn, which I loved to honk with the tenacity of a two-year-old boy. The memory always begins with the BEEP! BEEP! of the horn, followed closely by the ominous sound of a sliding door being pulled back. Then I look up from my tricycle seat and see a bellowing white-haired giant towering overhead. I know now that he was under the influence of Alzheimer's. In its early stages, it makes its patients irritable. But the understanding doesn't change the memory. It can't stop his rage.

I do have physical memories, though, photographs of him in the family albums. Every few months I pull them out and look at them. This was my grandfather when he was still in control of his faculties, alive and loving. But he is not full of life enough to do what I long for him to do — to shoot a gaze out of those photographs, to look across two decades into the frightened eyes of a little boy with a much bigger body and comfort him once more, a single precious glance to offset the one horrible memory that Nature in her cruelty chose to leave me. My grandfather's ironic last will and testament, funneled through my memory: I hereby decree that my grandson, Mason John Cole, though he bear my name and though I love him tenderly, shall be forced to remember me as a horrible ogre and/or a lifeless, inert vegetable (choice to be made by recipient) for the rest of his natural-born days. And may God have mercy on our souls.

After thirteen years of mental decay, my grandfather died. My father delivered the eulogy at his funeral, mercifully balanced this time with a few dark clouds to offset the sunshine and lollipop commentary: a funeral oratory that described a man who actually lived. I gave permission to publish a poem that I had penned about my grandfather on the back of the funeral program. It was so flowery that even Hallmark would insist it be rewritten. I hated it, because it didn't describe my actual feelings about the guest of honor — it showed him as I had never known him, as a man. Everyone else loved it. "How beautiful," they said. "You do remember him. What a sweet tribute." It made me feel like the worst kind of liar. They were accepting my fiction as their truth.

But I really have no truth about him. The closest I can come are the (thankfully infrequent) nightmares. You see, there are some nights when I do lie in that hospital bed and see from his eyes. I look at myself and realize we're not so different, after all. Then I wrap his arms around me and pull my struggling body into the bed, which turns into a closed coffin with the smell of death. After that I'm in my own body again, struggling against his cold dead hands, but never breaking free. And above it all I hear his voice as I always imagined it, deep and mournful: "I'm so sorry...so sorry...."

Perhaps the saddest irony of all is that I can't look out of his photographic eyes to see myself on the other side of the picture frame. Only his diseased eyes are mine to share. Most people remember their grandfathers with joy; mine has been my bogeyman.

Until recently, I thought he might fulfill that role in real life, as well. Scientists have proven that Alzheimer's has a genetic component to its makeup, with descendants of Alzheimer's patients being the most likely to get the disease. It would be the final sign that I was, indeed, my grandfather's grandson: his icy, clammy grave hands coming from the depths of nightmares one fine night to steal my most precious possession — my mind.

But recent research in the field of medicine — news that suggests a possible breakthrough against Alzheimer's will be made in the near future — fills me with a sense of hope. I have lived for several years with the fear that I will be doomed to follow my grandfather into mental oblivion, those seamy depths that my imagination has already visited too often. I have refused to accept his greatest gifts — his courage, his love, his ability to work — because

I have been afraid that in some way, it might obligate me to accept everything he offered me. But now it seems at last that there is a loophole in this ironclad contract. Maybe I can escape my ancestors, after all.

Perhaps, someday soon, science will indeed find a cure for Alzheimer's. On that day, I will finally be free — free to leave the shadows of the kingdom of the blind, the place where my grandfather ended his days and the obsession of my darkest nightmares, with not just a single eye, but also my full sight intact. With God's grace, I will never stare lifelessly at the seed of my seed, unable to recognize him, and haunt his dreams.

The Briefcase

Rafael Muñoz

I think I was the only kid in my hometown who actually liked wearing a suit. While other kids could not wait to jump out of their suits and put on jeans and t-shirts during church or holidays I happily wore mine for as long as I could. I once told my mother that my suit was more comfortable than my pajamas. In school I toned it down, but only a little bit, and wore an oxford shirt, with khaki pants or some other slacks. And, of course, what would become my trademark? My penny loafers (I had worn them ever since kindergarten). In a world of jeans, t-shirts and sneakers I stood out like a nudist marching on 5th Avenue on a snowy winter's day. I liked to dress like this, and most of my classmates were shocked that this was my choice, that my mother had not made me put on these clothes. Knowing this, it was no surprise to anyone that at the beginning of my fourth grade year I walked into the classroom with a briefcase instead of a backpack.

There are not too many things that I remember about my fourth grade year, but the day I got my briefcase is still alive in my memory. I had just returned from CCD and was ready to begin my homework: a math sheet on fractions, a couple of pages in *Dear Mr. Henshaw* and some verb conjugations in my grammar book. I took my books out of my bag, laid them out on the dining room table and got started. I was excited because it looked like I would be done before dinner, which my mother was busily preparing in the next room. I knew that if I finished I could play video games with my friend down the street. I was halfway through my math problems when I heard my dad walking up the driveway. He was talking to someone and they were both laughing heartily. I put my pencil down, ran out to meet him and realized that he was talking to Joe.

Joe O'Brien is one of the nicest people I have ever met. He was just like a big kid full of rambunctious energy and an impish smile. Joe told exciting stories and always surprised me with candy or a small toy that he would pull out from his pocket. You could say that he was my Irish Santa Claus. He was younger than my father, had just gotten married and did not yet have a family of his own. I think he almost saw me as his nephew.

When Joe saw me coming out of the house, he looked at me and said, "Hey, Buddy! Que se diche, my friend?" (this was his adopted Italian greeting). He picked me up and gave me a big bear hug. He put me down and, reaching behind the door of his truck, he pulled out something big and held it behind his back. He said, "I got something for you that I'm sure you'll really like." I kept trying to peek behind him but Joe wouldn't let me catch sight of it. He told me to close my eyes and hold out my arms, and then he handed me something light, wide and smooth. I opened my eyes and became filled with the joy of Christmas Day. It was the greatest present I had ever received: a briefcase. Even though it was made with fake leather, was a bit beat up and the material on the corners was starting to fray, I liked it all the more. Like Joe, it had character.

I opened it up, put papers inside and carried it around for the rest of the afternoon. I was so occupied with it that I forgot that I had wanted to play video games with my friend. I felt like a secret agent and imagined that the briefcase contained important government documents that had to be delivered to a secret location. If I failed in my mission an evil organization would succeed in blowing up the world. Before I went to bed, I put everything that was in my backpack into my briefcase and placed it next to my penny loafers so that it would be ready for the next morning.

When I arrived at school I was eager to show off my briefcase. I soon found out that, of course, none of my classmates held it in the same regard. They made fun of it and called it silly. They couldn't understand why I would want to carry around an adult thing like a briefcase instead of a new Ninja Turtle backpack. I fell back on my standard defenses; I told myself I didn't care. Besides, the kids at my school had always made fun of the way I dressed. I'd heard countless lectures on how I should wear sweatpants, jeans and sneakers like all of them did. I never listened then, so why should I listen now? I carried my books in that briefcase for the rest of the school year. The brown leather got even more worn out as the year went on and, perhaps, so did I.

When I entered fifth grade something changed. On the first day of school I walked into my new classroom, all dressed up (as always) and carrying my brown briefcase, which by this time had some duct tape to secure one of the handles. As I approached my desk I heard Charlie laugh at me. Then Tommy said with a smirk, "I thought you would've thrown that thing out by now." The rest of the week I faced the same type of comments from others, but unlike before they started to hurt more than they ever did. I used to be able to brush them off so easily, but somehow I started to think that maybe they were right. Why was I dressing this way when no one else did? And so I became tired of being different, tired of being made fun of, tired of not having anything in common with anyone else. For the first time I felt insecure and decided that once and for all I would try to be like them. That meant putting away my briefcase and buying new clothes. I asked my mom to take me to the mall, where I bought baggy jeans, a pair of white Nike sneakers and a Red Sox baseball cap. Until that year I would never have seen myself in jeans and, most shocking of all, a baseball cap for a team I was never even interested in. From this moment on, I conformed to what others saw as the norm. It made things easier; after so many years of sticking out I could finally blend in. I did so from fifth grade through high school.

When I look back at my life so far, I realize that there are often events that represent or mark key changes in our characters. Putting the briefcase away represented one of those events. My worn-out friend was a symbol of my individuality, what made me different from everyone else. In the fourth grade I was proud of my uniqueness, the clothes I wore and my ability to defend my own choices. Now that I look back, I feel foolish that I became ashamed of it.

It is interesting that now, in college, I am trying to recapture the individuality and confidence I had in fourth grade. In a small way I am going back. I've traded in my jeans for slacks; the shoes I wear, although not penny loafers, are no longer sneakers; and you won't find me wearing a baseball cap just because everyone else does. The change is not yet complete. That briefcase held something inside that I am still searching for.

Cultural and *Textual Analysis*

81

The Various Forms of Like

Brendan Vuolo

"It's like really, like, bad to use the word 'like.'"

What is wrong with this sentence? One observation may be that the word 'like' is misused twice. Another observation may be that whoever made this statement is a victim of the "like disease." The word 'like' has become so prevalent in our language that it often goes unnoticed. It is no longer specific to a certain minority of people, but instead it infects all people of ages ten to thirty. This disease is, of course, highly contagious, and once infected the victim has little chance of survival. The question that baffles everyone from English majors to English professors alike is: will there ever be a cure to this disease, or is language as we know it doomed forever?

To truly understand a word, we must first look at the origins of it. The word 'like' cannot be pinpointed to one exact source. Many people credit the California Valley Girl of the 80s for its modern implementation. Like has always been a common word in our language, as it has several definitions. However, we have gotten to the point where it can be many parts of speech at various points in a sentence. Whatever the original source may be, the constant use of the word 'like' is often thought to be indicative of adolescent speech. However, with time, these adolescents grew older and have become young adults in society. Unfortunately, many have not shed the "like habit." As expected, new generations of adolescents have picked up the word and use it regularly.

The question is, if our parents are of the "non-like" generation, then how do we become victims of the "like-disease?" The way we speak is more nurture than nature, so what is the explanation for this colloquial nightmare?

The answer can be found in television and most forms of mass media. Since the advent of television, each generation has become more and more influenced by the media. Stations such as MTV have been especially influential for Generation X-ers. Unfortunately, young people see MTV personalities as the models of being cool. It is, therefore, only natural for young people to imitate the way these personalities act, dress and speak. It seems impossible to watch MTV for a period of thirty seconds without hearing the word 'like' used improperly at least once (and that is the least of its grammatical transgressions). MTV's audience members will likely adopt MTV's improper use of 'like' because they are bombarded by its constant misusage. The proof that mass media shapes the way young people speak is that most six-year-olds will not overuse the word like. This is because child programming is purposefully grammatically sound. Eventually, peers start to influence speech more than parents, and the "like disease" has its foot in the door.

The word 'like' serves many purposes for adolescents. It can become a crutch for those who are unsure of what to say. Traditionally, a speaker may pause at this moment and think about what to say next. The word 'like' allows the conversation to never stop, even though it is not truly progressing. In this fast-paced society a pause in any form might seem odd. Naturally, any word may fill this transition; it just so happens that the word 'like' is a popular choice. I realize that I am equally dependent on the word. When, in mid-conversation, I am at a loss for ideas, I will repeatedly say the word 'like.' Then I stop and realize what I have done and try to be more conscious of it. Generally, though, it seems virtually impossible to escape the clutches of the word. It becomes instinctive. *automatic?*

As a member of Generation X, I believe that nothing is really important. If we go or stay, win or lose, pass or fail, it's all the same. It can all be shrugged off with an indifferent, "eh." It seems that no one will ever commit emotionally to avoid too much vulnerability. This apathetic attitude carries over into our speech, as well. If we preface any statement with the word 'like,' we are in effect covering ourselves in case the response is wrong. This is, of course, not grammatically or socially acceptable, yet every individual in this age bracket is a victim. If what we say is not accepted by others, then we can say we never really said it. We only said the answer is something like that. If the answer is correct then we will forget entirely that we used the word 'like' and bask in whatever praise we receive. It's a common trick used by many adolescents. A similar crutch is the phrase, "just kidding." I have noticed that many times students will follow an answer by saying, "just kidding." Or, if the answer is incorrect, the student will say, "Oh, just kidding. I meant...." Of course, the student was not kidding, and it is foolish to try to play off a wrong answer as a bad joke. However, this tactic is used by many people to prevent themselves from ever being wrong.

When we examine the entire English language we can see that the "like disease" exemplifies an informal way of speaking. The origins of this laxness can also be traced to the internet. When I was a sophomore, I remember my English teacher saying that people were making abhorrent grammatical errors, such as not capitalizing the word "I." At the time, I was shocked that people could make such a seemingly obvious mistake. However, I can now see that in three years this decaying of the English language has increased tremendously. Online, almost every word is abbreviated, if an abbreviation does not already exist. My repertoire includes the likes of "def." for definitely, "btw" for by the way and, of course, "jk" for just kidding. This kind of abbreviated and informal speaking online has now penetrated into our everyday speech. The word 'like' is similar in that it makes our everyday speech more informal.

Older people who were not exposed to the "like disease" might consider the misuse of the word to be very coarse. Conversely, most adolescents think excessive use of the word 'like' is no big deal. To the "pre-like" generation, misusing the word is sloppy or a poor way of representing oneself. Whenever I had to speak to an adult, my mom would say, "make sure to avoid saying 'yeah' and 'like'." I would try to follow this advice as much as possible, but this was impractical. I know that it made me look less polished and less professional, but it had become an involuntary habit.

Before we figure out how to banish the word like from our everyday speech, we must figure out what exactly it has become. Is it a verb, an adjective or both? I personally use it mostly as a verb. Instead of saying, "And then he said," I can say, "He was like." I have often realized the error of my ways, but then continued to use 'like' because I actually thought that it fit into the situation better. It has come to the point where a real word seems contrived and 'like' is actually preferable. Most often, 'like' is used for emphasis. It provides just enough of a pause to build suspense for what the next breath will bring. At the same time, it stresses the word that follows. Obviously a word that can function as so many different parts of speech must be kept for its value, if not for its uniqueness. But many would argue differently.

So what is the cure for this disease? I believe that this word will likely become more and more prevalent in our everyday speech, and that, as each generation passes it on to the next, those who do not use it will be a rare minority. It seems as if there is no way to consciously avoid saying the word 'like,' as it can be used so often. Worst of all, these new forms of the word like have infiltrated into the final frontier: the dictionary. Using 'like' as a verb is now not only socially acceptable but grammatically acceptable. It's safe to say that this is just the beginning. The best that the English language can hope for is that it becomes a somewhat-accepted word in all the various parts of speech that it encompasses.

Through Oliver Stone's Looking Glass

Kimberly Magee

The Presidential motorcade winds through downtown Dallas, weaving among a throng of onlookers, all hoping to catch a glimpse of the esteemed young Catholic. His open-air limousine approaches the corner of Houston and Elm streets and the book depository looms above (flash to clock). As the parade rounds the corner the convertible slows (flash to clock), the President waves (flash to clock), the first lady smiles (flash to clock) and someone fires. BANG. The motorcade stops dead in its tracks as more shots ring out. How many? From where? Who? Why? The President's head jerks back, then left and he is gone.

In perhaps one of the most confusing moments in American history a beloved President was assassinated. A tragic tale enraptured an entire nation with a few quick moments that would change the direction of the twentieth century. Out of the confusion, thirty years after the event, Oliver Stone presents a film meant to solve the mystery. Yet Stone generates his own brand of confusion, creating a film that is the epitome of movie manipulation. Stone uses a fast pace and many different media of film — historical, black and white, and color — in order to blur the line between fact and fiction and to manipulate his audience into believing a conspiracy theory.

Perhaps the most important factor driving *JFK* is pace, the rate at which a scene is played. Although over three hours in length, Stone's film moves rapidly. Stone uses an abundance of information, many characters and the quick thought process of his main character, New Orleans's District Attorney Jim Garrison, in order to speed up the pace. Right from the start, the viewer is inundated with information about the events surrounding JFK's assassination, from the parade in Dallas to scenes involving witnesses, citizens and future conspirators. Each scene depicts different characters, the majority of whom come back later in some capacity. The abundance of facts and characters not only serves to supplement and create the plot, but also to quicken the pace of the film because of the rapidity in which each scene is presented. Towards the beginning of the film, each scene is short, filmed in almost snapshot style, giving no more information than necessary. The movie moves quickly from one place to the next, one character to the next. With the abundance of information thrown at the audience, Stone does not give the viewer time to decipher between what events are historical, what events are fictional and what events are Garrison's assumptions. Stone uses the fast pace of the film in order to confuse the audience, making it difficult for the viewer to engage actively with the information he presents. Therefore, the viewer must accept all of the information at face value in order to follow the complicated plot and conspiracy theory.

Part of Stone's creation of perplexity is his use of different media, which serve to confuse the viewer's sense of fact and fiction. In the first forty-five minutes of the film, Stone creates scenes in two ways: in black and white historical footage and in color film. In the film's opening sequence Stone fluctuates between black and white footage of President Dwight Eisenhower's farewell address, John F. Kennedy's campaign and election, the Cuban Missile Crisis and Vietnam Conflict, and color re-creations of Jim Garrison's life and pursuit. The difference between the two media is clear and precise. The historical footage is real and in a black and white, grainy, documentary-style film. The color footage is the recreation of Jim Garrison's life. The two media of film never overlap or switch subjects: Jim Garrison is never shown in black and white, and historical footage is never in color. But this clarity does not last for long.

About a quarter of the way into the film, a pivotal scene changes both Stone's choice in media and the audience's involvement in the plot. Garrison, the New Orleans' District Attorney, and his colleagues sit down to dinner at a restaurant, each prepared to share the information gathered about the odd circumstances surrounding the Kennedy assassination. Susie Cox begins the conversation, presenting biographical research of Lee Harvey Oswald. Cox presents the information at such a quick pace that the audience cannot question its veracity. While Cox speaks about events in Oswald's life, childhood photographs of Oswald flash across the screen. The viewer believes these images to be actual pictures of Oswald, although the viewer has no way of knowing whether the photographs are real or not. Because of Stone's presentation of the information, the audience has no choice but to believe in the truth of both the photographs and Cox's statements.

As the scene progresses, visual images in black and white support the information Cox presents. For instance, as Cox speaks about Oswald's journey to Russia, the viewer watches black and white footage of actor Gary Oldman (as Oswald) renouncing his United States citizenship. Again, the viewer must assume that both the information and the footage are real because the oral word is supported by visual images. Stone's use of black and white manipulates the viewer into believing that the events and footage are historical, based primarily on the precedent Stone has set earlier in the movie. Stone uses the first section of the film to teach the viewer that black and white is historical footage and color film is the recreation of Jim Garrison's life. When Stone presents information about Oswald in black and white, the viewer recalls this precedent.

This scene is the first of many occasions during which Stone overlaps the conversation of characters and the visual images of other events. For instance, while Cox speaks about Oswald's possible link to the CIA, because of his facilitated re-entry into the United States after having defected to the USSR, images of a developing black and white photograph flash on the screen. The image of Oswald is pieced together visually as the conspiracy theory is born orally. In the visual plot, the image begins with a hand cutting out a silhouette, followed by the actual developing process of the photograph. In the aural plot, Cox and Garrison piece together Oswald's connection to the intelligence agency while the visual image of a man holding a gun becomes clear. Finally, Oswald's head is placed onto the photograph by an anonymous hand. At this point, Garrison deduces that Oswald may have just been a patsy, and that perhaps the Warren Commission's report may not be quite what it seems. The viewer believes that the photograph (which finds its way onto the cover of *Life* magazine and condemns Oswald in the eyes of the public) is fabricated, and thus the viewer also believes Garrison's deduction: that Oswald himself is a fabrication and is not the lone killer, or perhaps not a shooter at all. By forcing the audience to listen to the information being presented and to Garrison's conclusions, while watching an entirely unrelated scene, the viewer is left no time to decipher between factual and fictional information. Stone presents images while Cox speaks in order to support Garrison's assumptions, although strict attention to the actual evidence may not bring about such conclusions.

In perhaps the most powerful moment of the scene, Garrison tells his colleagues: "Y'all gotta start thinking on a different level like the CIA does. We're through the looking glass here, people. White is black, and black is white." From this point on, Stone overlies fact and fiction through the use of different media of film. The clarity of earlier scenes disappears as the lines between black and white and color, which were once used to decipher between fact and fiction, are muddied. The placing of Oswald's head onto another man's body is an image of this transition: someone has placed fact onto fiction to create Oswald, much like Stone lays fact onto fiction to create a conspiracy theory.

An example of this overlay of fact and fiction occurs when Stone recreates Garrison's late-night conversation with suspect/informant David Ferrie on the night of Ferrie's death. In the movie, a panicked Ferrie contacts Garrison because he needs to talk. They meet in a hotel room, where in rapid-fire succession Ferrie confesses to everything he initially denied. He tells Garrison that he does indeed know Oswald (whom he trained to shoot JFK), supposed CIA Operative Clay Shaw, the Anti-Castro Cubans and the assassins. He also tells him intimate details of the plot, finally confessing that the whole group works for the CIA. Following the conversation, Ferrie returns home, only to be found dead in the morning. In reality, the last person known to speak with Ferrie was a *Washington Post* reporter, who claims that Ferrie was calm during the interview (Epstein 89). Stone creates the hotel room scene in order to tie together the loose ends of his case: Ferrie links the Cuban shooters in Dallas to Oswald, Ferrie and Shaw, and furthermore links everyone to CIA. Ferrie, the Anti-Castro Cubans, Clay Shaw and Oswald all live, but all are not necessarily involved in the assassination. Stone combines the fact of their existence with the footage of Ferrie in the hotel in order to link all potential conspirators together, creating his conspiracy theory.

This overlaying of fact and fiction is not unusual as the film progresses. Garrison's quotation further symbolizes the conflict between fact, fiction and clarity: "White is black, and black is white," literally and figuratively. Black and white film is no longer only used for real, historical events. Instead, like the images of Oswald in the USSR, black and white film is used for many different types of scenes: historical events, Garrison's assumptions, events for which there is no record and witness testimony. Thus, Stone is able to continue to manipulate his audience through biased recreations and inventions of events, such as the David Ferrie confession.

Following the events at the restaurant there is no clear division between scenes in color and scenes in black and white, but there is also confusion between black and white and color within scenes. In the minutes immediately following the pivotal dinner scene, Stone presents a barrage of witnesses from Dealey Plaza where JFK was shot. One of the witnesses claims to have been whisked away by the CIA following the assassination and told that she never heard shots from the infamous grassy knoll. In a flashback to the event, the woman watches JFK's motorcade approach. As this scene unfolds, the woman describes the occurrences to Garrison. Up until the moment JFK is shot, the scene is shown in color. Following the shooting, the only color element in the scene is the witness herself, wearing a bright red raincoat. Like the tampered picture of Oswald in *Life*, this scene has been interfered with and color has been added. Stone shows how easy it is to tamper with evidence and reality. By adding a color element to a black and white scene, Stone confuses the viewer's sense of reality and makes it more difficult for the audience to determine the validity of the information presented.

Stone creates confusion in the previous scene in order to blur the lines between fact and fiction, as well as to show the viewers the ways in which the CIA confused the witnesses of the assassination. In the flashback, as the CIA pulls the witness aside and tells her that there were no shots fired from the grassy knoll, Stone shows how the CIA tampered with both the witness testimony and the witness's reality. The viewer does not know if the CIA's intimidation of the witness is real or fictional because of the confusion in the film technique. The witness comes away from the event unsure of what occurred and not knowing whether to believe her own senses or the CIA's stories. Likewise, Stone's viewers are confused, but they believe Stone's presentation of the "facts."

In addition to tampering one witness's sense of reality, Garrison proposes that throughout the Warren Commission Report the CIA and FBI tampered with evidence. A second female witness testifies to the CIA that she saw Jack Ruby in Dallas immediately before the assassination. The witness explains that as she was driving through Dallas she saw Ruby in a parked pickup truck. In Stone's recreation of the event, the witness's actions on the day of the assassination are shown in black and white. When Jack Ruby appears on the screen, he appears in color — the only color element in an entirely black and white scene. The Warren Commission reports that the witness could not identify Jack Ruby as the man she saw in Dallas. In addition,

Garrison proposes that the authorities forged the witness's signature and authorized the testimony. The audience does not know whether or not the Warren Commission report actually states that the witness could not identify Jack Ruby. The general audience does not have knowledge of the Warren Commission Report, nor time to pull apart Garrison's ideas, nor the ability to instantly verify the images Stone provides.

Film is primarily based on the audience's sense of sight, and every director of every film uses vision to his advantage. Movies have a tendency to suck viewers in, making them believe in the story, the characters, the theme and the plot of the motion picture. Every film attempts to master the art of manipulation in order to achieve the goal of a memorable movie: one that does not allow the viewer to live outside of the screen for the duration of the flick, one that leaves the viewer questioning and contemplating long after completion. Stone uses black and white, in combination with historical footage and color to manipulate his audience and blur the line between fact and fiction. By combining different media into one film, Stone makes it impossible for the viewer to distinguish between fact and fiction because he visually creates confusion. Following the dinner scene in which he first blends media, his technique confuses the audience. The dinner scene is pivotal because it is the point at which the movie changes: black and white and color are mixed, and Garrison's beliefs begin to dominate the film. The audience is only able to see the film through Garrison's eyes and Stone's creations. As Garrison develops his theory, the audience is dragged along with him. Stone's manipulation of the viewer facilitates the progression and, for the duration of the film, the viewer lives inside Garrison's mind, believing what he believes. Only after the film, when the audience is given a chance to think, to process and to digest what has been said and shown, does the viewer realize that all is not necessarily as it seems, that Stone has taken the viewer "through the looking glass...."

Works Cited

Epstein, Edward J. "The Second Coming of Jim Garrison." The Atlantic 271.3 (1993): 89.

A Penny Saved is a Penny Earned

Rebecca A. Magnone

I't's round, practically flat and takes up too much space in everyone's wallet. With edges slightly ridged and a permeating smell of metal, this coin is like no other. It is the message board for slogans on which this country is based: "E Pluribus Unum" and "In God We Trust." Yet Mr. Lincoln never looks us straight in the eyes, and he is simply a spot forever lost in the vastness of the Lincoln Memorial on the opposite side. What other object could better epitomize America today than the penny itself?

One may think it farfetched to describe three grams of copper as a symbol of society, but there is much more to the penny than meets the eye. The penny itself is rooted in tradition dating back to the days of Dickens in England. While all of the other United States coins are our own invention, we stole the penny. This coin also contains the face and the home of one of — if not *the* — most important, historical figures of our nation: President Lincoln. It is also the only coin made of copper. Obviously, the penny is a distinct piece of American culture and tradition, yet our society says it is worthless.

Why exactly is the penny considered useless? So extreme is this sentiment that people simply throw pennies into the trash. Here we are in a money-hungry society, where more is always better, and yet we throw money away. This may be confusing to some, but it actually makes perfect sense. People are shallow; people think they're too good for pennies because they can't understand the true value of things. This not only pertains to money, but also to what's really important in life. If more human beings could realize that having material goods isn't the key to happiness, we'd live in a much better society. Tossing pennies is just another way of displaying how Americans throw money away on a daily basis, whether it is on houses, clothes, cars or any other material object used only to impress others.

In recent years these objects that we use to show off our social status have only become more elaborate and more expensive — to the point where a penny can no longer purchase anything. It is interesting to point out this devaluation of pennies. The reason they spend ages in our wallets is that their only use is to make change. Value is not simply the ability to make purchases, but also the significance held in society. This failure to recognize value ties back in with a lack of respect for tradition.

Americans live and die by the phrase "out with the old, in with the new." We go around ripping down our Boston Garden to build bigger and better, leaving our country with no history. Is it not true that anyone will choose a shiny new penny as opposed to an old one that's been beaten down by the years? Shiny pennies are the downfall of American society. The reason that we choose the shiny over the rusty is that we are obsessed with appearances. We live in a world where women starve themselves, men use drugs to gain muscle and we spend millions of dollars on clothes that will be sitting in the backs of our closets by the end of the year. We get plastic surgery, change our hair color and pay exorbitant amounts of money for jewelry, shoes, cars and teeth-whitening treatments. The reason that we do all of this is not for ourselves, but so that total strangers will approve of our appearances. Do you honestly believe that the rusty penny is offended when the shiny one is chosen over it? We've gotten to the point where this problem is so bad that we even care what our pennies look like.

Hopefully there is still a small minority of people who believe the penny is not worthless. While most people disregard the one cent they save in a $1.99 purchase or a $99.99 item, it would be more beneficial to them to understand the true value of a penny saved *honestly* being a penny earned. To better emphasize this point we look to John D. Rockefeller, the king of Standard Oil. When he was building up his empire in the early twentieth century he made a very important business decision. Sealing his barrels of oil required ninety drops of wax per barrel, and each drop cost one cent. He simply altered this arrangement so that each barrel would use only eighty-nine drops of wax, and because of this he saved a million dollars a year. That's a million dollars in pennies, a hundred million pennies that symbolize the possibilities that we have as American citizens.

It would seem, then, most advantageous to understand what our penny has to offer. For years people have discussed getting rid of the coin altogether, and yet it still hasn't happened. The reasons for this may be varied. It could be due to laziness, no one person wanting to take the initiative or put in the effort to accomplish this task. Maybe flipping to decide seems too unprofessional. But I am of a different opinion. Think back to a time when you weren't yet corrupted by materialism, when you still appreciated traditions and it didn't matter if you were covered from head to toe in mud. Think back and remember the exhilaration of scrounging around a parking lot in search of those same coins that later in life would simply just fill space in a wallet. To find just one penny was a success, an elated experience. It is a feeling that no one can take away from a child, not even a society that's turned its back on the penny. In each penny collecting dust atop dresser drawers are both the pitfalls and possibilities of society. It's up to the owner of the jar to decide which side of the coin is better.

Research, Inquiry *and* Documentation

97

Subversion in the Culture of Signs

Michael Brady

The average city street is home to a gallery of images and messages designed to make a lasting impression on your mind. Set against the sky, gargantuan billboards hawk their wares while below, the sides of buses and taxicab roof-racks transmit similar messages to the teeming masses down in the trenches. Corporations are waging a war for the dollars in the pockets of the pedestrian. These businesses aim to make their products the most desirable. They don't want to be what you need; they need to be what you want. The increasing spending power of the American citizen has made these businesses more competitive, seeking newer, more visible ways to appeal to a person's eye. Advertisements have literally become fixtures in the American landscape. They pervade the culture, inhabiting every form of mass media communication.

There are many who fear the growing saturation of advertising in the world, and worry about the influence advertisers and corporations can have in a society run on capitalist ideals. These people see the often euphemistic and deceptive methods of marketing utilized by corporate America as damaging to the mind. They wish to create a place in society where a person can express his or her ideas without being drowned out by the "commercial cacophony" ("Culture Jamming"). These social activists participate in what is known as culture jamming. The goal of culture jamming is to provoke thought in the public through various methods, both legal and illegal, and to encourage an examination of the meanings and strategies behind the advertisements we see every day.

The term "culture jamming" was coined by experimental sound artists Negativland, who released the album *Jamcon '84* on SST Records. SST

Records was a haven for independent artists in the 1980s. The label attracted many artists who wanted to create their music on their own terms, without the interference of major record labels. These artists often touched on issues that were critical of American government and culture, things that would have been unwelcome on major music labels. SST band The Minutemen wrote songs about U.S. involvement in Latin America, the emptiness of pop culture and methods of marketing, declaring: "Let the products sell themselves! / Fuck advertising! Commercial psychology / Psychological methods to sell should be destroyed" (The Minutemen).

On *Jamcon '84*, Negativland first used the term "culture jamming," modifying the term "jamming," which meant to disrupt or make it difficult to communicate by CB Radio. The mission statement of culture jamming, according to the group, was to "add pimples to the face on the retouched cover photo of America" (Whelan). An effective and successful jam is one that exposes the true message behind an advertisement. It strips away the layers of carefully constructed images and euphemisms, turning the advertisement on its head. "[T]he incredible barrage of messages that invite us to consume [is our] number one environmental problem" (qtd. in Motavalli), according to Kalle Lasn, co-founder of The Media Foundation, a group dedicated to culture jamming. Statements like these may seem drastic or hyperbolic, but one must first look at the methods and motives of marketers, and the effects they can have on people, before judging the truth of Lasn's words.

The goal of any advertisement is to persuade or cajole individuals into believing they must have the product. Advertisers frequently employ methods that attempt to guide a person's tastes in order to create demand for products where currently there is none. Developing brand recognition and loyalty between consumers and companies is extremely important. "To accomplish this covenant," says James McNeal, author of *The Kids Market*, "brand marketing must start with children. Even if the child does not buy the product, and will not for many years — AT&T services, IBM computers, Sears appliances — the marketing must begin in childhood" (qtd. in Signorelli). Studies show that children begin to recognize the stylized logos of brands at about eighteen months. By age two, they begin to ask for products by name, and a year later they begin to compare one brand to another. McNeal says that by first grade a child is conscious of over 200 brands, and companies able to achieve recognition at this stage "are able to secure nearly unshakable customer loyalty" (qtd. in Signorelli). Brands such as The Gap, Old Navy,

Polo and Harley Davidson have developed product lines for children in an effort to find a foothold in the burgeoning consumer demographic. In an interesting twist, Ford Motor Company recently unveiled a full-size truck, co-branded with the Tonka brand, in order to appeal to the adult consumers' nostalgia for a successful brand imprint given to them in childhood. Children today have more spending power than ever before, and have in front of them a diverse marketplace with countless brand products to choose from. Winning over key demographics is essential to the success of a company.

Culture jammers argue that the methods employed by advertisers in order to win over young children are detrimental to their development. When children are bombarded with advertisements designed to shape their opinions from birth, how can they learn to think analytically and form their own opinions? "I like to be trendy because it aids in my social skills," says seventeen-year-old Jonas Jacobson. "[Being trendy] makes me feel confident and helps me interact with people" (qtd. in Baum). Jonas is a teenager from an upper middle class area of Boulder, Colorado. He is the perfect example of someone who has been successfully branded. His loyalty to brands such as Abercrombie & Fitch, American Eagle and Structure are secure because of his beliefs that the clothing helps him to blend in, making social interaction easier. Dan Cooper, director of the online style magazine *Fashionfinds.com*, believes that Jonas is the perfect example of most of the Abercrombie-wearing adolescent public. "Most young people are anxious about themselves and their futures, and many are depressed. What you see from the likes of the Gap is what young people would like to be." However, Cooper does not believe that this method of marketing creates an atmosphere of confidence. "What they are actually accomplishing is creating an Orwellian vision of a world where everyone has to be alike" (qtd. in Baum).

The seeds for these trends are planted throughout mass media. WB television show *Dawson's Creek* has a product placement deal with American Eagle, which wardrobes every character on the show in their apparel. Advertisers play on adolescent insecurities about their self-worth or self-esteem and use them to more effectively market their products. Furthermore, brands such as Abercrombie & Fitch and American Eagle display their brands prominently on their apparel, effectively turning their consumers into advertisements. These visible and invisible pressures dissuade teens from finding their own voice or style, and inspire conformity and acquiescence. As the old Gap advertisement says, "Everybody's in," and there is little room to be different.

This type of mental and emotional manipulation, which often is not as explicit as in Jonas Jacobson's case, is what drives culture jammers to subvert the methods of marketing.

While the targets of most culture jamming activities are large corporations and their advertising campaigns, the goal is not some lofty anarchist pipe dream about bringing down capitalism. "What we're trying to do is pioneer a new form of social activism," says the Media Foundation's Kalle Lasn (qtd. in Motavalli). The Media Foundation is the organization behind *Adbusters*, a quarterly publication that deals with advertising and cultural issues. Through *Adbusters*, which has a circulation of 85,000, the Media Foundation organizes such resistance events as "Buy Nothing Day" (November 29) or "Turn Off Your TV Week" (April 22-28). They also display spoof ads for products like Absolut, featuring the taglines "Absolute Impotence" and "Absolute End," complete with statistics on drinking-related car accidents. The Media Foundation also produces thirty-second television messages dubbed "Uncommercials." These spots twist everyday advertisements. One features an attractive, semi-nude woman in what looks like it could be any fashion advertisement, until you realize that her undulating is caused by her vomiting into a toilet. "The beauty industry is the beast," it declares. CBS, NBC and ABC all refused to air paid advertisements for "Buy Nothing Day." The Media Foundation was more than willing to pay the going rate, just like any other organization seeking to advertise on television, but the anti-corporate subject matter was seen as unfit for television.

Other organizations take parody and advertisement subversion to great lengths. Perhaps the most high-profile of all culture jamming activities is the "liberation" or "modification" of billboards, as practiced by groups like the Billboard Liberation Front. The BLF began in 1977, when Jack Napier and Irving Glikk (pseudonyms), altered a Max Factor Cosmetics billboard to read: "A PRETTY FACE ISN'T SAFE IN THIS CITY — FIGHT BACK WITH SELF-ABUSE — THE NEW MUTILATOR — AX FACTOR." What started out as a prank blossomed into an adventurous hobby that has spanned over twenty years. Since its inception, the BLF has undertaken dozens of billboard modifications in an effort to disrupt the negative messages transmitted by advertising. The BLF's manifesto states: "It is clear that He who controls the Ad speaks with the voice of our age" (Billboard Liberation Front).

Before its eventual banishment from advertising billboards, the tobacco industry was a frequent target of the BLF. A large neon billboard, featuring Joe Camel and the words "Camel — Genuine Taste," was modified to read "Am I Dead Yet?" In 1989, following the Exxon Valdez oil spill, a San Francisco billboard reading "Hits Happen — The New X-100" was changed to "Shit Happens — The New Exxon." Apple Computer's 1998 "Think Different" campaign, which featured famous figures like the Dalai Lama and John Lennon, was attacked, leaving images of Amelia Earhart with the message "Think Doomed." The Apple campaign, according to Napier, is "a great example of how absolutely everything, no matter what it meant in different circumstances, can be used as a sales model" (qtd. in Chun).

In 1997, the BLF superimposed the face of Charles Manson over a psychedelic Levi's advertisement. In its press release, the BLF addressed issues of cheap labor and marketing strategies in a mocking tone. In addition to its obvious mass-market appeal, the decision to employ Manson as spokes convict speaks directly to Levi's fastest-growing demographic: the burgeoning worldwide prison population. Assembled by prisoners in China, sold to penal institutions in the Americas, this blue-denim sub-market saturation demonstrates complete back to front, top to bottom market integration" (BLF).

Though they have some critics, the BLF also receives praise from many corners. *Utne Reader* nominated the Billboard Liberation Front as one of its ten media heroes of 1991 (Chun). The BLF does its best to alter boards without doing serious damage to the property, and often leaves a pack of beer behind as a gift to whomever is given the job of restoring the billboard to its original state. "We don't have anything against billboards," says Napier. However, I'm miffed at that idea that wealthy individuals and corporations have access to drive-by media. These are very expensive to lease or rent or own" (qtd. in Chun).

While the BLF seeks to engender some critical thought about advertising media through its actions, other groups do view billboard modifications as a direct attack on a marketing culture that values profit over people. Pedro Caravajal, a culture jammer who works with a mostly Latino group called Cicada Corps, targets the disproportionate number of advertisements for alcohol and tobacco products in low-income minority neighborhoods. The motives behind these modifications are altruistic, and Caravajal says the residents in the neighborhoods he visits are thankful to the Corps, often offering to help mix their wheat paste or lend them a ladder (Chun). Another method of defacing advertisements, known as skulling, comes from a feminist critique on the images of women portrayed in culture. Using nothing more than a magic marker, Toronto performance artist Jubal Brown showed people how to draw on the faces of the ultra-skinny fashion models to create a deathly, ghoulish skull. Skullers take the bulimic ideal of beauty as portrayed by the fashion and advertising industries one step further, leaving a skeleton to sell you Lee jeans.

Corporations are usually vigilant in protecting their logos and trademarks, but when it comes to culture jamming, many fear the battle. While many actively ask police to crack down on trespassing violations, they rarely bring the cases to trial. Many jammers would love the chance to engage a corporation in a legal battle. Corporations fear that the cases would be fought on political grounds, led by culture jammers who are acutely aware of the effect media attention can have on a company's bottom line. In 1992, Absolut Vodka dropped a suit against *Adbusters* over its alcohol parodies when *Adbusters* challenged Absolut to a public debate on the harmful effects of alcohol ("Culture Jamming"). Ignoring the problem seems to be the best way of dealing with the issue of culture jamming. In 1997, Negativland released the album *Dispepsi,* which mangled and maligned Pepsi jingles and ad campaigns. The album contained lyrics such as "I got fired by my boss / Pepsi/ I nailed Jesus to the cross / Pepsi / The ghastly stench of puppy mills / Pepsi." The official Pepsi Co. response to the album was that they thought it was "a pretty good listen" ("Culture Jamming").

Another method of diminishing the activities of culture jammers was used in a 1994 campaign for the Plymouth Neon. The original billboards featured just the car against a plain white backdrop, and the text "HI." In the following weeks, the advertising firm modified the billboard to read "HIP" or "CHILL" in what was meant to appear like spray paint. In retaliation, the Billboard Liberation Front further modified the billboards to read "HYPE," and added "666." Napier says of the incident, "Eventually advertising will consume all methods and modes of communication, and they'll regurgitate it like a rat consuming its own bowels" (qtd. in Chun).

Culture jamming serves an important role in our society, bringing attention to the sometimes-duplicitous meanings behind the images and experiences we encounter every day. They inspire people to think carefully about their purchases and to examine the advertisements they see with a critical eye. American culture, based on ideals of freedom of speech and expression, is being overpowered by the concepts of commercialism and consumerism, where trends and ideas are formed in the minds of advertisers and sold to the public. Writer Umberto Eco sums up what he calls "semiological guerilla warfare": "The receiver of the message seems to have a residual freedom: the freedom to read [the symbol] in a different way.... I am proposing an action to urge the audience to control the message and its multiple possibilities of interpretation" (qtd. in Rheingold). Culture jammers are disrupting the passive acceptance of the signs and symbols presented to us in order to create a more open, more aware culture.

Works Cited

Baum, Gary "The New Teen Image: Marketed, pre-packaged, and sold at a
store near you." *The Cherub Crier.* 24 July 2000
<http://www.medill.northwestern.edu/specialprograms/nhsi/2000/
abercrombie.html>.

The Billboard Liberation Front. *Billboard Liberation Front.*
<http://www.billboardliberation.com>.

"Culture Jamming: Ads Under Attack." *Brandweek* (10 July 2000): 28.

Chun, Kimberly. "Free the Billboards: Billboard Liberation Front Guerilla
Campaign." *Gadfly Online*
<http://www.gadfly.org/archive/issues/isses-billboard-7-01.html>.

The Media Foundation. *Adbusters.* <http://www.adbusters.org>.

The Minutemen. "Shit from an Old Notebook." *Double Nickels on the Dime.*
SST, 1984.

Motavalli, Jim. "Culture Jammin': The Media Foundation combats excessive
· advertising." *E* (May-June 1996): 41.

Rheingold, Howard. "Culture Jamming." *Whole Earth Review*
(Spring 1994): 100.

Signorclli, Lara. "Branded For Life?" *Christian Science Monitor* (1 Apr 2002).

Whelan, John. "The Mayhem is the Message." *MetroActive.* 1995
<http://www.metroactive.com/cyber/jamming.html>.

Protest Music of the Vietnam War:
A Struggling Generation Moved to Action

Elizabeth A. Vassallo

Radio host George Jellenik once said, "The history of a people is found in its songs" (qtd. in *Pacific Northwest, Blues in the Schools*). Bob Dylan; Crosby, Stills, Nash and Young; Phil Ochs; Creedence Clearwater Revival; Joan Baez. No other era of musicians could have created a nation's history quite like this in America during the Vietnam War.

In 2001, almost four decades later, this same music of the 1960s is still proving its timelessness. Thanks to my dad and our family's frequent trips from Maryland to New York, I cannot remember a time when this music was unfamiliar to me. The New Jersey Turnpike at midnight, the tight quarters of a station wagon's backseat and the soft crooning of Bob Dylan coming from an aged tape deck — all key parts of our family trips. Little did I know then, as I watched the changing scenery through the window, that the songs which for me simply made the hours on the road go by more quickly meant the world to an entire generation who came before me.

The lyrics and influence of 1960s musicians were truly revolutionary in that they not only sold albums but also took a firm stance in the state of society itself. The protest music created during the struggle in Vietnam was much more than a soundtrack for an era of war. It was a response to injustice, a protest against violence and ultimately a call to change that united Americans during the conflicts of a struggling generation.

The struggles all began with a war most citizens did not understand in a land unknown: Vietnam. The government's goal of U.S. involvement in Vietnam was to keep South Vietnam anticommunist. Achieving this goal meant finding and destroying Viet Cong and North Vietnam army units, and potentially killing thousands of innocent Vietnamese citizens and American soldiers in the process (Loss 75).

For the sake of the U.S. government's mission in Vietnam, more than two million men were drafted into the military by the U.S. Selective Service System and even more voluntarily enlisted in hopes of getting favorable assignments (Hillstrom and Hillstrom 112). My uncle was thirteen years old when the turbulence of the Vietnam War began and just eighteen when, in 1972, he was drafted into the army. Of the young American men drafted to fight, close to 58,000 died in battle and an additional 270,000 were wounded (101).

My dad was fourteen years old when the casualties of the Vietnam War began to accumulate. "The most striking memory," he says of wartime, "is not so much the progress of the war, but some of the pictures which looked cruel and ugly." Even today, my dad recalls a time when each news broadcast was ended with an update of how many Americans had been killed that day and to date. My uncle describes the same time period: "You would eat your dinner watching film footage of the war, seeing film footage of people dying."

It is no wonder, then, that as young people like my father grew up they began to protest the violence that for them symbolized the conflict in Vietnam, what my dad and his contemporaries viewed as "another country's civil war." Protests of the war grew also to concern the disproportionate amount of citizens from the lower classes of American society represented in the army. It seemed that, as Kevin Hillstrom puts it, "Vietnam was a place where the elite went as reporters, not as soldiers" (112). It is a known fact that many affluent young men were exempted from the draft because they had hopes of higher-level academic achievements in the future. Members of the lower socioeconomic classes were at an academic disadvantage and, as a result, ended up comprising a majority of the United States' drafted armed forces (112).

Youth disgust with the war and the way the government was dealing with it only grew with time. "Primarily, the War in Vietnam seemed unwinnable and poorly thought out," says Carol Petillo, history professor at Boston College and teacher of a course on the struggle in Vietnam. "Most college students," she continues, "did not want to die there along with the other 58,000 Americans who did. It [the war] became more and more unpopular as it went on."

Clearly, though, the Vietnam War, awful as it was, could not have been the first "unpopular" conflict to see U.S. involvement. What was it about the time and the circumstances of this war that made so many American citizens speak out during the 60s and 70s? Essentially, the young people of these decades could take a stand because their path of American protest had been paved long before the war even began. Years preceding the war, an era of change was sparked by former President John F. Kennedy's move to office as the youngest president ever elected. Kennedy's enthusiasm and willingness to question the traditional, combined with the mounting Civil Rights Movement, created a whole new era. In essence, "the complacency of the 1950s was over" (Denisoff 194).

Furthermore, the call for protest was beginning to foment society. "The assassination of a popular president; ghetto riots; an escalating war in South East Asia; freedom rides; all perplexed observers of American Society. College students were in the eye of the storm" (Denisoff 194). These college students, likely children of veterans of World War II, were raised during a period when society truly believed in the principles of the U.S. government. When these same students grew up to see the government "not living up to those expectations," as Professor Petillo puts it, they spoke out and began questioning the very thing they had always been taught to trust without doubt.

Thus, the anti-Vietnam War movement found its roots and soon after found life in the music of American folk singers. Joan Baez, Bob Dylan and Phil Ochs helped to make protest music a key part of the antiwar movement of the Vietnam Era. Rooted in slave songs and union ballads, the protest song quickly became a revolutionary form of "artistic journalism," thanks very much to the work of singer, songwriter and poet, Bob Dylan.

Dylan, with his 1962 album, *The Freewheelin' Bob Dylan,* is credited by many for having single-handedly founded music's antiwar movement. The songs on this album, and many of Dylan's songs to follow, allowed him to take his place as a "spokesman of his generation." Former President Bill Clinton credits Bob Dylan with "providing those who protested the Vietnam War with a moral compass as accessible as the nearest radio" (qtd. in "Voice of America"). Clearly, though, Bob Dylan did not speak out for his generation on his own, but rather was aided by many other musicians who also decided that it was time to truly speak up to their contemporaries and to the world.

Musicians all over began to take a stand. John Lennon asked society in a simple but powerful way to "give peace a chance," while others made more direct attacks on the government and on the conflict itself. "Be the first on your block to come home in a box," sing Country Joe and the Fish in their wartime hit of 1967, the "I-Feel-Like-I'm-Fixin'-to-Die Rag." In Creedence Clearwater's 1969 single, "Fortunate Son," John Fogerty makes a statement on the injustice of a war fought by the American middle classes (Hillstrom and Hillstrom 112). "Some folks are born silver spoon in hand...Some folks inherit star spangled eyes," sings Fogerty. "They send you down to war and when you ask them, how much should we give, Ooh, they only answer, more, more, more" (qtd. in Armstrong).

In a time of emotionally explosive issues in America, "contemporary popular music," says Les Cleveland, "[became] related directly to the passions and anxieties of an entire generation of people to the point where, in the hands of the peace movement, it became a political tool (qtd. in Walsh). The music made society ask "why?" and as protests of the Vietnam War grew, "songwriters seized the moment," as Les Cleveland puts it, "to express the anxiety of the day and mobilized the troops on college campuses across the land" (qtd. in Walsh).

Students for a Democratic Society, founded in 1962, was one of the most influential organizations in rallying American college and university students in support of the antiwar movement. Its major goal of returning the United States to its "original ideals of participatory democracy" sparked many young Americans to action (Loss 76). When the powerful public protesting began, my dad was one student at Columbia University in New York City who actively took part in the protest, marching down Broadway with hundreds of other students for the sake of the cause. He recalled a time when students went as far as taking over the college's administrative buildings. These Columbia students proceeded to close down the school.

For students like these across the United States it was contemporary protest music that proved to be what my dad calls "another medium for the message of social awareness to be spread." The music became the uniting force behind many protest groups and demonstrations. John Fogerty once said, "I think music, my concept of what music is supposed to be...should unite, as corny as that is" (qtd. in Hillstrom and Hillstrom 116). And unite the music did. American citizens from California to New York were coming together with the help of antiwar music.

Even Americans fighting overseas in Vietnam felt the influence of that same music of the time. Songs like the Animals' "We Gotta Get out of this Place" became extremely popular among soldiers because the lyrics touched them personally as citizens who were sacrificing for a cause so many simply could not believe in. Many protest songs became "anthems" for soldiers everywhere because, heard from the jungles of Vietnam, they "reflected their feelings of disillusionment, homesickness, anger, and pain." The music was one source of media that the military had difficulty controlling. It became a key link between the young people fighting the war and the young people supporting them back home in the United States (Hillstrom and Hillstrom 292).

The influence of the music during this period on civilians and soldiers alike is undeniable. But did the musicians behind the music always intend to "change the world" with their lyrics, or were they just selling albums to naive teens? Neither. It is easy to forget that musicians like Jimi Hendrix, David Crosby, Neil Young and John Lennon are not just symbols but members of the generation that survived the Vietnam War. David Crosby says in Johnny Rogan's biography, *Neil Young,* "I don't think musicians should go and seek stands out.... But when something slaps you in the face personally, you have to respond to it" (qtd. in Hillstrom and Hillstrom 214). Musicians were men and women who were living through and responding to their world in the best way they knew how.

Crosby, Stills, Nash, and Young's famous song "Ohio" is a testimony to the very fact that the musicians were living the struggle along with the rest of society. In his autobiography *Long Time Gone,* David Crosby describes the night Neil Young wrote the song "Ohio," following the shootings at Kent State University. Crosby recalled watching Young read a magazine article about the shootings and then simply look up "as if to ask 'Why?'" Young then sat down and, in silence, wrote the song that would soon be heard across the nation. "It was a true life reaction of one young person to the world he was living in, a time of great controversy and conflict," says Crosby (qtd. in Hillstrom and Hillstrom 214).

Maybe it was the fact that the music did embody "true life reactions" to the conflicts of society that made the music of this period so powerful. Or maybe it was merely the circumstances under which the music was created and heard. But, for whatever reason, the protest music of the Vietnam War had a powerful influence that outlived the struggle itself. The protest song did not go away after the war, but instead "adapted, changed to suit the time" (Walsh). Though in many senses, antiwar music of today is less unified, with-

Crumble ?.

out a lone cause, the music continues nevertheless and remains pertinent and applicable to the conflicts of today's society. During the Persian Gulf War, for example, modern musicians such as Lenny Kravitz, L.L. Cool J., Tom Petty and Sean Lennon came together to rework and then perform John Lennon's historic "Give Peace a Chance" at the United Nations (Sullivan).

While many other songs of the Vietnam era are redone, new socially-conscious songs of the modern era are also being created. U2, for example, protests conflicts of Northern Ireland in "Sunday Bloody Sunday," the Clash criticizes American interventionism in "Washington Bullets" and Jackson Brown mourns the fates of Nicaragua and El Salvador in "Lives in the Balance." Singers like ex-Pink Floyd leader Roger Waters and Randy Newman also continue to create music pertaining to the struggles of our modern world. Bruce Springsteen is another figure who has done the same through his 1995 hit, "Born in the U.S.A." (Sullivan).

Since I was ten years old, I have known the words to songs like Bruce Springsteen's "Born in the U.S.A." and Bob Dylan's "Blowin' in the Wind." I would sit in that back seat of our station wagon, with its fake wood peeling off the outsides and coffee stains embedded in the seats, and sing along for hours. "How many roads must a man walk down? ...Dad, can you turn it up, please!" I would yell. And he would laugh as he probably thought back to the first time he heard the song. Such different worlds the two of us lived in when I was very young. The times are always changing, though, and they change more quickly than one might think.

Today, at age eighteen, I find myself in a similar position to the one my dad must have been in just under thirty years ago. Both smart, young kids on the brink of our college experiences; both thrown into a world that is often far from the ideal; both trying to figure out where we fit into the big picture, my dad and I do not seem so different anymore. Whether the struggles we face are those of the Civil Rights Movement and the Vietnam War or those of radical terrorism and the anthrax virus, the same questions apply.

Bob Dylan asks, "How many times must the cannonballs fly, before they're forever banned? ...How many deaths will it take till he knows, that too many people have died?" (Bobdylan.com). No matter what era we live in, the same music that united an entire generation of Americans during the Vietnam War can be applied as we face and are changed by the struggles we live through. Some things might simply never change, and maybe the answers to those timeless questions of justice and peace asked by Bob Dylan and so many others will forever be "blowing in the wind."

Works Cited

Armstrong, Muriah. "Fortunate Son (J.C. Fogerty)." 12 Nov. 2001
    <http://clps.kl2.mi.us/stwork/history/muriahly.htm>.

Bobdylan.com. 15 Nov. 2001 <http://bobdylan.com/songs/blowin.html>.

Denisoff, R. Serge. "'You Know Something's Happening, But You Don't
    Know What It is Do You Mister Jones?'" *Sing a Song of Social Signifi-
    cance.* Bowling Green, Ohio: Bowling Green State University Popular
    Press, 1983. 190-8.

Hillstrom, Kevin, and Laurie Collier Hillstrom. *The Vietnam Experience, A
    Concise Encyclopedia of American Literature, Songs, and Films.* Westport,
    Connecticut: Greenwood Press, 1998.

Lonergan, William. Telephone Interview. 10 Nov. 2001.

Loss, Archie. *Pop Dreams — Music, Movies, and the Media in the 1960s.* New
    York: Harcourt Brace College Publishers, 1999.

Pacific Northwest, Blues in the Schools. 7 Nov. 2001
    <http://bluesintheschools.org/history.html>.

Petillo, Carol. Telephone Interview. 13 Nov. 2001.

Sullivan, Jim, and Steve Morse. "Hell no, peace songs won't go away."
    Editorial. *Boston Globe* (25 Jan. 1991): 43.

Vassallo, Joseph Anthony. Telephone Interview. 6 Nov. 2001.

"Voice of America; At 60, Bob Dylan is still his generation's troubadour."
    Editorial. *Pittsburgh-Post Gazette* (23 May 2001): A-24.

Walsh, Jim. "Vietnam gave birth to protest song." *Times Albany (Albany, New
    York)* (29 Apr. 2000): D7.

Isabella

Jonathan Fabbro Keephart

The hollow sound of a sniper's rifle broke the serenity of the morning mist. I arose from my short rest without any reluctance. I was beyond tired; my body did not feel sleepless. Instead there was a numbness among my extremities that mollified the cold, hard advances of the outside world. I could not remember at what time I began my rest, but I never forgot to wake up from it. Perhaps my subconscious reminds me that every extra minute I lay in dream, I am that much more susceptible to the sudden assaults of the Russians. The taste of peppered meat lingered in my mouth and I crawled over to my satchel for some sourdough. I crouched low as I made my way over to it, and it became apparent that both trenches were now awake and active.

I sat, legs crossed, in front of my grandfather. My eyes were transfixed on his as his pupils fluctuated with the inflection of his voice. I dug my fingertips into the soft beige carpet, exploring the texture of the fabric underneath the fibers. He took a sip of his wine and continued.

Bullets whizzed over my head every few seconds. By now, the event did not faze me as it had in the past. The Russians were fairly accurate with their rifles, so when a round whistled above my head it meant that they were shooting close; but when I heard a loud snap nearby, it was clear that I was the intended target. I wasn't being shot at yet this morning, and I wasn't too worried as I positioned myself at my post. My duty was to man a fifty-caliber machine gun that I nicknamed Isabella after my girlfriend, who was equally loud and destructive. I reached around the gun and cupped my hand as I dragged it over the sandbags that were protecting me. Cold, misshapen pieces of metal dropped into my palm and I carefully reeled my arm back towards me. I counted forty-seven of these wretched little rifle rounds and dropped them into an old helmet sitting beside me. I usually found more bullets stuck in the bags from overnight, but winter had begun and concern shifted to conserving body heat, as opposed to taking pot shots in the dark. I was well accustomed to being fired at and I considered myself a relatively critical target.

From sunrise to dusk, I strafed the area in front of me, affectionately known as "no man's land." Out there, icicles hung off the rusted barbed wire that lined the ground in no identifiable pattern. Men trying to cross into the opposing trenches with grenades had cut much of it during the night; nevertheless, the remaining amount was enough to stop any man literally dead in his tracks. The soil was riddled with craters from mortars and I could see small black needles of mines that had been set underneath the surface. All in all, to make it past the wires without getting diced, or to run over the holes without breaking an ankle, or to hop over the well-concealed mines and not be blown to smithereens were formidable tasks. And yet, men tried every day. Now, one was running laterally across my plane of view and I let off about three seconds worth of ammo at him. A line of bullets hit the frozen ground and kicked up little pieces of dirt near him before he arched his back and was retired from the action. He tried to get off a few more steps and tossed a grenade about ten yards ahead of him before falling harshly on his face. His head bounced severely as it met the cruel ground and his helmet slid upside down toward the grenade. The two met briefly before they lost momentum and the grenade refrained from detonating. The soldier joined the ranks of thousands before him who were cut down in search of glory. Unfortunately, honor, pride and courage provide little protection from a hail of machine gun fire. The corpses of these idealistic men were evidence of heroic attempts made in vain.

My grandfather shifted in his brown leather recliner. The arms of the chair were worn and revealed a softer, lighter layer of material that reminded me of that old bomber jacket I had seen my father wear in photographs as a youngster. My grandfather gave me a little smirk before he went on to acknowledge my impatience for the story to proceed.

I scanned the distance with an old scope and tried to look over the edge of the other trench. The tops of the helmets looked like shells of snapping turtles breaking through the water's surface. I looked to see if the gunner opposite me was in position yet. He was, and I could see his blood-stained helmet peeking above a mass of sandbags and piles of dirt. There was probably four-helmets-worth of material composing his own and it was all taped together with a dirty beige-colored cloth. He was also looking through his scope and we both knew we were looking directly at each other. He put his hand up quickly and pulled it down, acknowledging me, and I did the same. I did not know this man, but I could see that he was young like myself, no older than twenty. Perhaps at some other time, some other place, he might be the kind of guy I would buy a beer and chat with about past girlfriends. Now, though, we were supposed to be enemies, and whether or not I forgot that, he would still kill me if the chance arose.

Something moved in the distance and I turned and opened fire. I stopped quickly as I realized that it was just a dog scurrying across the wasteland. Its paws slid sideways as it struggled to keep its balance on the ice. Its grayish fur blended in well against the dreary scenario and I wondered if it felt as lonely as I did. I stared for a couple of seconds but, regaining focus, I looked through my scope again at the other trench. Oddly, I sighted about seven or eight heads peeking above the edge of the trench with binoculars pointing toward the dog. I wondered why such a benign creature was attracting so much attention; the focus in this trench was still on things capable of shooting munitions. I turned the scope on the canine and saw that it was making its way toward our mortars. I looked closer and noticed a pouch tied to the belly and neck of the animal that nearly hit the ground when the dog's feet slipped. A small antenna poking out of the bag made me shudder as I realized what was in it. "Jesus," I sighed. "The damn thing doesn't even know." I wheeled the barrel around and unleashed a small torrent of gunfire onto the unsuspecting animal. Instantly, a large detonation sprayed ice, soil and entrails within a few feet of the mortars and the soldiers that manned them. I turned Isabella towards the other line and fired until the jarring backfire made my teeth hurt. My hands and arms tingled fiercely from the vibration while the rotating barrels kept spinning smoothly. We used to call Isabella the kaleidoscope not because of her spinning barrels, but because of what we suffered when we first began to use her. Soldiers would say that, after a few minutes of continuously firing the hellish machine, they would be so disoriented from the vibration that they would see colors and hallucinate. I got over this pretty quickly, though, and I was glad that my good aim prevented me from running in conventional infantry. I'd been there for three weeks and there were only six people left that I recognized.

I ducked down and looked back into my scope. I looked where the eight men were watching the dog and noticed some fresh blood there. This part of the trench was not very far from me, so I assume that I may have taken out three or four of them while they were stunned from the premature explosion. I scanned farther down the trenches at my opposite in battle. I could not see the creatively reinforced helmet any longer and the man's gun was pointing towards the sky and to the left. I followed the metal down and I saw a gloved fist clenched around the grip. The wrist was twisted in an uncommon position and I wondered what provoked him to hold on while below surface. Suddenly, a set of white hands grabbed his wrist and tugged hard. His grip did not loosen and the hands pulled his fingers from the grip. His fingers stayed grasping as his arm fell limp from view. Another man quickly donned his helmet and pulled the gun back into a firing position.

"Ankommend!! Ankommend!! Gefahr!! Ankommend!!" shouted a drove of men running from the mortars through the narrow earthen corridor. I recoiled down below Isabella and covered my face as I braced for what I expected to be an uncomfortably close barrage of mortars. I didn't hear the familiar whistle that accompanied the mortars, but instead I heard a struggling aircraft engine. I spread my fingers and looked to where the sound was coming from. A small olive-drab fighter plowed directly into the trench about thirty feet away and a piece of propeller sliced its way through the air towards me. It slammed into the old helmet beside me and I winced in pain as hundreds of disdainful bits of munitions careened upwards, pelting my face and hands. The barrage ended quickly and the minute assailants quietly rained down into my lap, chilling my thighs under their icy steps.

The severed prop was respectable in size and about the length of my thigh. Its black paint was chipped from the impact and it was bowed like a sliver of the moon. The crash had sent large chunks of frozen soil into the shattered cockpit and the remaining glass was crimson with spatterings of blood and brains. The pilot's head sat forward and his face had encountered the jagged canopy like a watermelon meeting a steel grate. There was little left of him to recognize except for the insignias that lingered on the side of the fuselage. I took shallow breaths and looked around me at the stunned faces of those still ducking nearby.

My amazement was short-lived and firing resumed from our side as men carefully crawled under the aircraft to get back to their weapons. I selected a section to watch and fired at intervals to discourage any valor from the other trench. I dug my foot into the dense soil and felt something on my toes that I hadn't felt since I left Sicily. My socks were saturated with some liquid, but it couldn't have been water; that would have frozen in less than a minute. I looked down in horror to see a river of fuel running from the fallen aircraft. I could not respond to this looming disaster before return fire sailed above and clinked against the exterior of the plane. The plane snarled and released a ferocious orange growl. The billowing fireball rumbled towards me and lit the petrol river like a carpet of flames. I bounded towards the other side of the trench in full stride. I was cognizant of the overhead ceiling of projectiles and I was not slowed by a pair of bullets plunging deep into my bicep. My agony was unfathomable as the fuel seared through my pant leg and boiled the skin from my calf like wax dripping from a candle. I fell into one of my compatriots and a flash of white stunned me before we both hit the ground.

"Leo...Leo...Leo, prego svegliate." I slowly opened my eyes and let in the abrasive light of the hospital room. My mother and Isabella were each holding one of my hands. Streams of tears ran down Isabella's tan cheeks and fell onto my forearm. She gasped for breath as she tried to speak between sobs. My father and brother stood with their arms crossed and tried to resist showing their elation through crying. My mother made the Sign of the Cross and repeatedly kissed my face and my forehead and my cheeks. I didn't say anything; I didn't have to. My eyes welled up and made everything blurry until my salty tears were released. They ran down onto my lips and I closed my eyes and continued to cry.

My grandfather pressed his lips together and his nostrils widened as he took a deep breath. I remained silent for a few seconds, too awestruck to respond in any verbal terms. The expression on my face was probably enough to sum up my reaction. That Saturday night, as my friends were gallivanting around town, stories of German trenches and allied fighter planes raced through my head. I wondered then what exploits I will have embarked upon when I tell stories to my grandson.

Hollow compared to the civilities of the narration

What Hollywood Doesn't Know About ECT

Barbara Breen

My mother met an angel that day. Had this assertion come from any one else, I would have promptly dismissed the person as an irrational religious zealot, but my mother had never said anything like this before. She doesn't believe in astrology and is skeptical of miracles. My mother *was* anxious that day; she had, after all, put her signature next to mine on a consent form allowing a doctor to perform a controversial procedure, electroconvulsive therapy, on her fragile fifteen-year-old daughter.

The angel approached my mother in the pre-operative room and began talking to her about the treatment and her own experience with it. My mother asked questions about her story. Everyone in a waiting room like that has a story. The angel had begun her battle with depression at the onset of puberty. Although she had signs of disordered eating, she was convinced this had been a way to gain some control as her depression had controlled her for years. She knew eating would no longer be a problem as long as the depression wasn't completely consuming. She had been receiving electroconvulsive therapy every few months for years in order to maintain the effect. The last thing she said to my mother was, "If I'd had ECT at her age, my life would have been completely different. I wouldn't have lost so many years."

Unless a family member or friend has been treated with electroconvulsive therapy (ECT), one may be more familiar with the term 'shock treatment.' One might recall the image of one of America's most beloved stars, Jack Nicholson, being fastened to a table with leather straps and shaking violently in the loony bin doctor's cold-hearted attempt to control the witty character. This was the scene in the 1975 film, *One Flew Over the Cuckoo's*

Nest. Or perhaps one has read Sylvia Plath's *The Bell Jar*, in which she retells her own experience with ECT in an autobiographical novel. The first account of ECT in the novel is a violent and negative experience, and few readers are willing to reconsider the humaneness of ECT by the time they get to the later, more positive experience (Smith). Although the recent movie *A Beautiful Mind* handled the subject a little more gently and allowed the viewer to accept the judgment of the psychiatrists who performed the treatment, the old ECT methods were still intact at the time Nobel Prize winner John Nash received the treatments. As a result, it is a chilling, violent scene.

These depictions allow the American mind to make assumptions about the treatment without ever knowing anything about the success rate or recent improvements in technique. Americans are given just enough knowledge to make a judgment, but not enough to be educated on the subject.

The angel's story was also mine. She was not in the recovery room and we never saw her again. Angel or not, she was exactly what my mother needed. It calmed her nerves to see someone so confident in the success of the procedure she was about to watch her daughter go through.

I, on the other hand, was not at all worried. It was the summer before my sophomore year of high school and I had already lost the spring to mental illness, not to mention my whole seventh grade and much of eighth and ninth. I lost track of my hospitalizations after number seven. They began to be a joke to me. I did not mind being there unless I knew I was missing something on the outside and, when I was, I knew just how to manipulate the situation to get discharged. I was magically better two days before my freshman semi-formal, and depressed again two days after. It was a system like any other, and as long as I knew how to work it, hospitalization could temporarily stabilize but never cure me.

Ugo Cerletti discovered ECT in the 1930s. Originally using chemicals, the method made the patient's body convulse, that is, have a seizure. Later, electricity was introduced, which allowed the doctor to pinpoint a specific place in the brain to receive the shock and experience the effects of the seizure. It is used to treat severely depressed, bipolar or schizophrenic patients, and recent studies have shown it to have between an 80% and 90% success rate, much higher than any medication available to treat these mental disorders. It is not completely understood why ECT is so effective, or even why it works at all. The neuroendocrine hypothesis suggests that the body's hormonal system is altered by the seizure, and the anticonvulsant hypothesis states that the brain's neurochemistry is altered during the seizure because of the brain's natural response to try to stop the seizure (Glass). The mysteriousness of the treatment may add to Americans' skepticism, as the educated American patient has been taught to be aware of her options and to be an active participant in her treatment decisions. It is not surprising that a dismissive "This will make you better, but don't ask why" would be less than satisfactory.

In the 1940s and 1950s, psychiatrists were excited by the prospects of treating mental illness successfully for the first time, but they didn't show good judgment in allowing patients to understand the procedure of ECT, nor did they carefully choose who was appropriate to receive this treatment. It was performed on the wrong patients, without formal consent, too many times. Furthermore, patients often suffered serious, unexpected side effects from the overuse of bilateral ECT. At this time, doctors did not use the muscle relaxants and anesthesia as they do now, and therefore bone fractures, bitten tongues and potentially traumatic memories of the treatment were additional side effects to those encountered today (Glass).

As for me, I was a fifteen-year-old with nothing to look forward to. I wanted to die. I had frequent happy moments, but they were transient and it was difficult to appreciate them when I knew it was only a matter of time before I would leave the sunshine and retreat back to my cave of dramatic poetry, painful music, temper tantrums (that seemed to have been stored up since I was two) and contemplation of an escape. I no longer wanted an escape from my cave; I just wanted to leave it all. I did not want to be part of a world where things could become so horrible. I had nothing to lose when I signed the consent form and walked into the treatment room. Either there would be an added sense of permanence to my "better" or I would die. Fifteen years old was young to see things in such a stark manner, and to have been doing so for three years. The antidepressants they had used to "cure" me numbered as many as the hospitalizations they had used to "stabilize" me, but I was neither cured nor stable. Worried about how long they could keep me safe and desperate to save their youngest daughter, my parents began asking about ECT. Doctors were skeptical about the amount of success possible with the remaining untried antidepressants, and I was tired of waiting. After much deliberation, it was decided I would receive ECT in June of 1997.

I was wheeled into a large bright room at Massachusetts General Hospital, where there were about five stretchers holding patients who had just received ECT or who were about to receive it. There was a divider between the patients waiting and the one being treated, but one could hear the murmurs of the doctor and nurses talking. Many of the patients, if not asleep, were incoherent and mumbling to themselves. My doctor specialized in the elderly, who had too many other health conditions to safely take antidepressants or antipsychotics. He had warned me they would be there and I should not worry about their condition being a result of the ECT; rather, they were receiving ECT to rid them of their delusional states. Dr. Welch had explained everything I would experience and the possible side effects. I strongly believe this preparation makes the difference between a good and bad experience with ECT.

My mother was with me the whole time and even watched my first treatment. I received intravenous anesthesia; the burning sensation as it penetrated my skin was the most painful part of the treatment, and I fell asleep within thirty seconds. From this point I do not remember the procedure until I woke up in the same waiting area with a horrible headache a half hour later. Even with Percocet, a strong painkiller, my head felt as if it were being continuously hit against a wall. I would go home after about twenty minutes, and would sleep off the headache and drowsiness from the anesthesia. In a scene that resembled nothing like the one in *One Flew Over the Cuckoo's Nest,* my mother said that the only movement in my whole body while the treatment took place was the wiggling of my toes. The doctor had explained to my mother that the muscle relaxant would not reach my toes, as to indicate to the doctors that the seizure had successfully taken place. The treatment was done within minutes, but the actual 'shocking' happened for less than a second. I returned to MGH eight additional times for treatment on Mondays, Wednesdays and Fridays over the course of three weeks.

Although the side effects of ECT are much less detrimental than they were in the past, patients and, in the case of the incompetent, the patients' guardians should be fully aware of what the treatment entails before signing a consent form. Short-term memory loss and even amnesia in rare cases have been reported as side effects, and patients often have intense headaches and/or a feeling of confusion after treatment. These side effects have greatly diminished since researchers have discovered that unilateral ECT, or the targeting of one hemisphere of the brain, is almost as effective as the traditional bilateral method. However, relapses occur much more frequently with unilateral ECT, and therefore this course of treatment is usually followed up with antidepressants and/or regularly scheduled maintenance ECT treatments. There are rumors that ECT can cause brain damage, but it has been proven that the amount of electricity that would have to pass through the brain to cause damage is significantly larger than that involved in ECT (Glass). A survey done by England's Royal College of Psychiatrists in 1982 found that out of 2594 treatments, four deaths occurred "to which ECT might have contributed." In only one of these deaths, however, was ECT thought to be the main cause (Fraser 73). For a disease, depression, with a mortality rate of nearly 15%, 0.2% seems tolerable (Glass).

The ECT affected my short-term memory for the period of the treatments and the following two weeks. I was unable to remember things such as arguments I'd had with friends, so I learned to keep an extensive journal to keep track; meanwhile, I had no problem remembering things like my phone number, which I had known for years. Much to the dismay of my doctor, I even took my English final, in an attempt to get it over with, on one of the days between treatments. My short-term memory is completely back to normal and, as I have shown in this narrative, I have recollection of the time surrounding the treatments.

The stigma attached to depression alone is incredible, let alone that of a controversial treatment of depression like ECT. People who do not understand depression often question the validity of the disease and wonder why patients do not just "pull themselves up by the bootstraps." Others believe that depression will pass or that it is merely a figment of the imagination. Few treat it with the seriousness of cancer. In reality, depression is a highly debilitating disease with a significant mortality rate, most of the deaths occurring by suicide (Glass).

Moreover, ECT is not conventional; sending electricity through someone's brain is not often used to treat disease. People are willing to swallow almost any pill a doctor prescribes to them in hopes of curing their ailments, but, and perhaps rightfully so, they are much more skeptical of allowing a doctor to perform ECT on them.

I received unilateral ECT and, although I do not remember much else, my research has brought me to a better understanding of the procedure. The burning in my hand from the IV was the administration of the short-acting barbiturate, and soon after succinycholine was administered to relax the muscles to a state of paralysis, preventing fractures while the seizure took place (Smith). The barbiturate and succinycholine make the difference in the level of humanity that is now available in the treatment. People are no longer tied down to tables and forced to experience the traumatic feeling of their bodies shaking uncontrollably.

In unilateral ECT, electrodes are stuck above the temple of the nondominant side of the brain and in the middle of the forehead. The electricity is then passed through the brain for less than a second while an electrocardiogram and electroencephalogram monitor the heart and the seizure activity, respectively (Smith).

In a survey done in 1980, 80% of the patients surveyed said that "having ECT was no worse than a visit to the dentist" and 65% were willing to have it again (Abrams 166). I have no regrets about having the treatment. Although I was young, I believe that my doctor, who interviewed me extensively about my depression and interest in ECT, knew that I was in no way being pressured or persuaded by my parents to undergo the treatment. It was clear that my mother and father had their reservations about the treatment, but they were in a desperate position. The doctor was also able to tailor my treatment to allow for my mother's presence during the procedure. The treatment itself, from my experience, is harmless. As long as the patient has qualifying indications and is fully aware of the procedure's side effects, I see no reason for there to be hesitation in the use of ECT.

In April of the following year, I experienced a relapse of depression. Although it never returned in the same severity as in the years before, knowing that ECT was helpful, I returned immediately for four treatments over a week and a half. My last treatment was on my sixteenth birthday and, after a long nap, I made it to my surprise birthday party. I do not know what would have happened to me had I not been treated with ECT, but do I know that this story might have ended differently. Much easier to say now that I have survived those dark years, I am thankful for the perspective my experience with depression has given me. Bad days are just bad days, no longer the end of the world, when you've seen a place so dark. I may owe the real credit, however, to the renowned doctors who have been perfecting this treatment for seventy years, because, without them, perspective would not have been enough help.

Works Cited

Abrams, Richard. <u>Electroconvulsive Therapy</u>. Oxford: Oxford University Press, 1988.

Fraser, Morris. <u>ECT: a Clinical Guide</u>. Chichester: John Wiley & Sons, 1982.

Glass, Richard M. "Electroconvulsive Therapy: Time to Bring It Out of the Shadows." *The Journal of the American Medical Association* (14 March 2001): 1346. *InfoTrac.* 22 January 2002 <http://web2.infotrac.galegroup.com>.

Smith, Daniel. "Shock and Disbelief." *The Atlantic Monthly Magazine* (February 2001): 79. *InfoTrac.* 22 January 2002 <http://web2.infotrac.galegroup.com>.

Argument and Persuasion

129

Morally Straight

James Noonan

"**O**n my honor, I will do my best to do my duty to God and my country and obey the Scout Law; to help other people at all times; to keep myself physically strong, mentally awake, and morally straight" (*Boy Scouts of America*). From third grade at my first Cub Scout meeting to my Senior Recognition dinner, I have heard and recited the above oath or some derivation. For nine years these words simply stood for righteousness. There was no questioning the morals this oath professed. These words never held a secret message that needed to be unlocked. A scout tried to be the best that he could be not just to benefit others, but himself, as well. Yet in April 2000, the words for the above passage took on a new meaning. The words "morally straight" had suddenly morphed into a description of sexual orientation. Morally straight, which once had stood for the attempt to be morally honest, had been twisted to mean the Boy Scouts were against gays. Somehow I had missed the message.

In nine years of scouting, the word 'gay' never came up in any official scout context. I had gone through all of the steps: the hikes, the merit badges, the advancement and finally the Eagle Award. It was only now, when I had peaked in my scouting career, that I began to encounter countless questions dealing with gays: What exactly is the Boy Scouts' position on gays? Why? What did they do to you? Questions about my involvement in scouts transfigured into pseudo-attacks. I had nothing to do with this sudden decision to change the message of the organization I had grown up in, and now I was held responsible for the decisions made by adults halfway across the country.

On April 26, 2000, the Supreme Court heard arguments dealing with the expulsion of the homosexual assistant scoutmaster, James Dale. Dale was a model scout who reached Boy Scouts' highest rank, the Eagle Award ("Boy Scouts – Discrimination"). After graduating from scouting at the age of eighteen, he volunteered to become an assistant scoutmaster, an adult who helps to run various scout functions. Dale came out in college and became involved in the gay community. When his local troop spotted him in an article in the Newark newspaper describing the plight of homosexual teenagers, they revoked his membership. When Dale asked for an explanation, the council declared that the Boy Scouts of America "specifically forbid membership to homosexuals" ("Can't a Scout Be Gay?"). Dale sued under New Jersey's Law Against Discrimination. At first, the New Jersey court ruled that the Boy Scouts had no right to oust Dale and ordered his reappointment.

The Boy Scouts of America then appealed to the federal Supreme Court. The Boy Scouts claim that accepting Dale as scoutmaster would violate their rights to free association. Though being gay is nowhere explicitly forbidden in the Boy Scout text, the passages in the Scout Oath and Law included excerpts that demand that a scout be "morally straight" and "clean." At the time they were written neither passage conveyed a sexual connotation — the term "straight" had yet to be associated with sexual orientation ("Can't a Scout"). In fact, these laws also contain passages that state that a scout must "accept ideas and customs different from his own," a law certainly broken by the Boy Scouts' stance on gays. The Boy Scouts, nevertheless, used these passages to show that the homosexuality went against their expressive interests as a "private" entity. In their interpretation, a homosexual is neither morally straight nor clean. Therefore, forcing the Boy Scouts to accept homosexuals would be sponsoring gay activity that goes against their specific expressive interests ("When the Boy Scouts Went Down"). This interpretation was accepted by five of the nine members of the Supreme Court when they concluded that the "group's ability to advocate their viewpoints would be adversely affected if they had to keep a gay scoutmaster" (Feldblum).

The decision by the Supreme Court has its obvious consequences for the gay community. Like James Dale, they are forced out of any involvement in the Boy Scouts organization. Besides ostracizing the gay community, however, the Boy Scouts of America are forcing scouts and former scouts like me to deal with the consequences. Not only do we undergo the interrogation of others but, perhaps more difficult, we scouts have to evaluate our position on the Boy Scouts decision. The Boy Scouts of America argue that "an avowed homosexual is not a role model for traditional moral values espoused in the Scout Oath and Law and homosexual conduct is inconsistent with values [Boy Scouts of America] wish[es] to instill" (*Boy Scouts*). In the recent Supreme Court case, the Boy Scouts, in essence, declared themselves an anti-gay organization.

Some are afraid that gay scout leaders are more likely to molest their scouts. However, both sides seem to recognize the fact that homosexuals are no more prone to molesting children than heterosexuals. In fact, the Boys Scouts long abandoned this argument. During oral arguments, Justice Sandra Day O'Connor asked the Scouts' lawyers twice if fear of child abuse was a rationale for the ban on homosexuals, and the attorneys answered in the negative both times. Therefore, the Boy Scouts ban has nothing to do with the actual protection of children but with the Boy Scouts' views that homosexuals are dirty and wrong. This is a direct hit against the homosexual community. Much like the Boy Scouts' argument that gay participation would be sponsoring homosexual activity that is inconsistent with the values they hold, scout participation in the Boy Scouts of America could be conceived as sponsoring the position of open discrimination against homosexuals.

While Boy Scouts has played a major role in my growth and adolescence, I currently do not approve of this outdated stance on homosexuals. However, my participation in scouts did not focus on the national leadership of Boy Scouts but instead centered on my local troop. Parents ran the adult leadership of the troop, fulfilling such roles as that of scoutmaster. If a child were discovered to be homosexual, the troop would attempt to deal with it in an open manner. So when the issue of gays in the Boy Scouts first came about, I felt no personal conviction towards the results. Yes, this decision is inappropriately discriminatory, but it had little influence on my local troop. I believed that I could live in seclusion from the effects of these decisions by the national administration, and I was able to do that for some time.

However, as the Boy Scouts cases began to pick up national interest, I discovered that I was becoming more and more affected by the backlash against the Boy Scouts. Whenever Boy Scouts was mentioned, the controversial gay issue was sure to come up. Soon people began to drop their support of the Boy Scouts, attempting to force the national administration to change their views. However, it was not the national management that reaped the consequences. Instead, innocent scouts found themselves caught in a windstorm that many of them failed to understand. Suddenly churches, various organizations and local governments stopped supporting the area troops. My troop now had to deal with whether the mayor would be willing to attend our yearly Eagle Court, while in years past we always hosted the area's representatives and local government officials. During this ceremony we also received letters of recognition from various famous personalities and high-ranking government officials. However, in the past two years, these letters have become harder to come by as more and more people feel the need to protest the Boy Scouts' anti-gay position.

More serious than letters and guests at ceremonies is the support of fundraisers that pay for troop activities and equipment. As the protest against the Boy Scouts continues to grow, our troop is going to have difficulty selling the wreaths that raise enough money to support our troop for the year. Such a decline in our fundraising limits the activities that the troop can be involved in. This loss of support has nothing to do with the actions of our troop but with the policy of the national organization.

Yet perhaps the most symbolic danger is the threat to our scout cabin, which has been in our possession since the troop's founding in the 1940s. The cabin is on local public ground and has slowly been encroached upon by a nearby school. In theory, they hold the land on which the cabin stands. A change in administration could now easily result in the loss of our cabin, the central location of our troop and the center of all of our activities.

My troop isn't the only troop dealing with the harmful effects of the backlash against scouts. Across the country support for scouts is dropping. The United Way is phasing out its support of the Boy Scouts. Even the national Boy Scout charter risked extinction when Rep. Lynn Woolsey introduced legislation to revoke the Boy Scouts' eighty-four-year-old charter. Even as scout troops attempt to adapt to the outbreak of action against the Boy Scouts, they are reprimanded by the administration for any attempt to bypass the anti-gay decision. If a troop declares a lack of bias towards gay scouts, the troop will likely face either an insistence that they abide by the council's policies or the revocation of their charter. This places troops and scouts at the mercy of the national administration. If they disagree with the administration's resolutions, the choice is between quitting and forcing the discriminatory practices.

For the sake of local troops and scouts, the national administration needs to alter its decisions regarding homosexuality. If they do not want to fully accept gays into the administration, they at least need to compromise, to find a stance in the middle. They could follow the action of the Girl Scouts, who have quietly forbidden bias against lesbians by insisting that leaders not display their sexuality in any way ("Boy Scouts – Discrimination"). Or they could follow the example of the Canadian or English Scouts, who have accepted gays. Until they do something, however, local troops and innocent scouts will have to continue to suffer the casualties of a political battle in which they have no control.

Works Cited

"Boy Scouts – Discrimination and the Law." *The Economist* (29 Apr. 2000): 29-31. *InfoTrac*. Nov. 2001. Gale Group. 11 Nov. 2001 <http://infotrac.galegroup.com/itweb/mlin_m_bostcoll?db=EAIM>.

Boy Scouts of America. Boy Scouts of America. 11 Nov. 2001 <http://www.scouting.org>.

Bull, Chris. "Fanning the Flames." *The Advocate* (22 May 2001): 48-50. *InfoTrac*. Nov. 2001. Gale Group. 11 Nov. 2001 <http://infotrac.galegroup.com/itweb/mlin_m_bostcoll?db=EAIM>.

"Can't a Scout Be Gay? The Boy Scouts' Battle to Stay Straight Goes to the Supreme Court." *Time Magazine* (1 May 2000): 34+. *InfoTrac*. Nov. 2001. Gale Group. 11 Nov. 2001 <http://infotrac.galegroup.com/itweb/mlin_m_bostcoll?db=EAIM>.

Feldblum, Chai R. "Moral Law, Changing Morals." *The Nation* (9 Oct. 2000): 22-3. *InfoTrac*. Nov. 2001. Gale Group. 11 Nov. 2001 <http://infotrac.galegroup.com/itweb/mlin_m_bostcoll?db=EAIM>.

"Why the Boy Scouts Went Down." *Gay and Lesbian Review Worldwide* (Jan. 2001): 15-20. *InfoTrac*. Nov. 2001. Gale Group. 11 Nov. 2001 <http://infotrac.galegroup.com/itweb/mlin_m_bostcoll?db=EAIM>.

Act 33: Children or Criminals?

Susan McGee

There is a portion of my mother's office, a corner nook, a sacred grouping of shelves engulfed in a heaping pile of wooden renditions of her name, skillful sketches of her countenance, letters of appreciation. My mother is a teacher. But not in the sense of apples and chalkboards and lockers and recess; her classroom is contained within the walls of a maximum-security county jail in Pittsburgh, Pennsylvania. My mother, a tiny woman, barely scratching the surface of five feet, spends a solid eight-hour day, five days a week, confined within the very same walls as rapists, serial killers and child molesters, and she does so with joy. There is no other way to describe it; she sees something in everything, maybe hope, which, coincidentally, is also her name. And the students never cease to amaze her; she beams at their accomplishments, but never forgets where her classroom is contained or the reason her pupils have been placed there. They are children, but they are also criminals.

My mother did not always teach at the county jail: her transfer from a juvenile detention center to her current place of employment came about after the birth of Act 33, an adult time proposal put into effect in 1995 by Pennsylvania Governor Tom Ridge. Under these new conditions, juveniles age fifteen and above can be charged as adults if they commit one or more of seven given offenses and perform these crimes with a deadly weapon. The offenses include aggravated assault in the first degree, robbery of a motor vehicle, arson, rape, involuntary deviant sexual intercourse, aggravated indecent assault, robbery offenses of the first degree, kidnapping and voluntary manslaughter. In addition to the execution of these acts, the conspiracy, attempt or solicitation to commit any of the crimes can result in adult jail time.

I find Act 33 to be both disheartening and pessimistic—an easy out for dealing with today's youth crimes. The message it sends is concise, yet immensely discouraging: juveniles who commit these seven offenses under the described circumstances are not shown a path toward a crime-free future, but rather are abandoned in a sea of life-long criminals. I can see that, in many cases, these violence-prone youths do not deserve the right to serve time with children who, more simply, deal drugs or cave into peer pressure. These criminals are not ones that embody hope for a transformed future; they have committed acts viewed so gravely that it is unimaginable that they have come from a child. Maybe such a child no longer has a right to love and understanding; maybe such a child should be left to flounder in a criminal environment. Maybe all that child will ever know is a jail cell, and possibly it should be that way. But it is difficult for me to imagine anyone locking away a face not even old enough to see an R-rated movie, and all the more difficult for me to believe that the life of a child is a failure at puberty, that he or she should no longer dream or put stock in any kind of a future.

My first major hesitation with the Act deals with the outline of the legislation itself; it is both too broad and too harsh, a dangerously inhumane combination. Instead, it should be targeted to specific, extremely violent circumstances. The only cases that should be passed along to adult court should be those of sickening severity, those without a hint of remorse in the teen's eyes, those committed with cold calculation, where redemption is virtually unimaginable. Only when the imprisonment of these unstable teens in a juvenile facility would mean endangering others should adult incarceration be considered.

Maintaining the broad circumstances instituted by the Governor only seems to put a damper on the hope of rehabilitation and suppresses the humanity in each of the delinquent youths. These children have done wrong by legal and societal standards, but they are still children, and their basic human needs must be met. When placed into an adult environment, these children are denied the opportunity to touch or kiss their mothers or grandfathers, to feel that they are loved and that rehabilitation would matter to someone. In juvenile detention centers, family plays a significant role in reform. What hope is there for a child to grow up to be an outstanding citizen when the role models of his or her youth have been murderers and thieves? These juveniles will simply learn the key to being better criminals, not better people.

What these young offenders truly need is access to quality therapy and instruction, which is much more readily available at juvenile-specific detention centers than in adult prisons. They need guidance away from the environment that fosters the malice and desperation of their acts, a push away from the mental anguish they clearly engulfs them. The juveniles who would commit crimes of such a serious nature most likely are not without social or mental disturbances, and need intensive psychotherapy. Such therapy holds a future: a glimmer of normalcy, a choice for a tomorrow.

Although I find much of this legislation to be destructive and inhumane, one specific aspect of Act 33 is absolutely atrocious. Until their verdicts are given, accused juveniles are held in an adult prison if they cannot make their bail. For a child who might eventually be found innocent, this time, sometimes up to a year, can cause unimaginable permanent damage. The poorest of juveniles fall into this trap; they have been raised in targeted crime areas and are more likely to be pinned falsely as criminals. Placing the at-risk children in a cellblock with the deadly and vulgar deviants of society can only fuel negative desires and breed aggressive resentment toward a seemingly unjust judicial system.

I wonder if there isn't a better way to salvage the delinquent youth of today. The passage of such legislation as Act 33, while seemingly effective on paper, creates a looming, bleak undertone in the way we view disturbed children. It sends out a message that they cannot be touched, that no amount of therapy can improve the outset of their lives, that they are innately criminal beings. This is not to say that the adult prison systems do not have their share of rehabilitation programs and complete turn-around cases, but children learn from their surroundings, and the atmosphere of a prison educates in terms of a prison culture, not one composed of the norms and ideals of the outside world.

There will always be certain individuals who, even at a tender age, possess the physical and mental traits to do real harm to their communities and to themselves. Maybe there are some people who simply cannot be reconfigured, that from the time of birth have hatred and malice pumping through their veins. All the same, more of an effort from state and federal governments toward rehabilitating the criminal youth of this country is necessary. Maybe I'm just foolish, or maybe I, like my mother, can see a little bit of hope in even the darkest, loneliest of jail cells.

Vegetarianism: A Higher Form of Living

Andrew Snopkowski

When I was in the third grade I grew curious about where the meat on my plate was coming from. I was also becoming suspicious about the ethical question surrounding the consumption of meat. It actually started earlier than that, though; according to my parents, I have been reluctant to eat meat since the age of three. They didn't really understand me at the time. In fact, one of my grandmothers always said I would one day meet a girl who was omnivorous and that I would change my eating habits. At first, I was simply repulsed and disgusted by meat; I didn't yet have the maturity to develop a more sophisticated reason for refusing to eat meat, fish or chicken. That all changed by the time I reached my teens.

I know now that there are several different types of vegetarians. There are vegans who eat only food that comes from plant sources; lacto vegetarians who eat dairy products (no meat or eggs); ovo vegetarians who eat eggs (no meat); and lacto-ovo vegetarians who eat dairy and egg products (no meat). There are also other distinctions of vegetarians like pesco (only fish) and pollo (only chicken) vegetarians; however these people are typically not defined as true vegetarians ("Different Types of Vegetarians"). I am, for the most part, a lacto-vegetarian; I eat dairy products but abstain from anything else. For this very restricted diet I get little or no support. My whole family eats meat and, since I can remember, so do every one of my friends. Most are not sympathetic and many actually think my eating habits are weird. It's sometimes a difficult life to live; there are not always a lot of food options, especially on a somewhat secluded college campus. It's also difficult because there are few people I know who share my ethical assertions.

I have come to realize, though, that I am not alone; many of the greatest minds in our history have abstained from eating meat. These famous vegetarians include Pythagoras, Socrates, Plato, Clement of Alexandria, Plutarch, Leonardo da Vinci, John Milton, Sir Isaac Newton, Voltaire, Benjamin Franklin, Jean Jacques Rousseau, Percy Bysshe Shelly, Ralph Waldo Emerson, Henry David Thoreau, Leo Tolstoy and Albert Einstein ("Famous Vegetarians," "People—List by Firstname"). Even if a person is not a vegetarian this list of names should draw his or her attention. Vegetarianism seems to be the way of the more enlightened mind. It is my feeling, along with those of the above individuals, that vegetarianism contributes to the best way to live life — it has substantial health, economic and, most importantly, ethical benefits.

Eating a diet that contains a lot of meat has proven to be significantly unhealthier than that of a vegetarian. Heart diseases and osteoporosis development is increased considerably by the consumption of red meat. According to the *Journal of the American Medical Association,* "Ninety to ninety-seven percent of heart disease can be prevented by a vegetarian diet" (qtd. in *All-Creatures.org*). Though many people question the lack of protein in the vegetarian diet, it has been discovered in the past decade that a person doesn't need that much protein in his or her diet. In fact, if people get most of their protein from vegetables they can lower their cholesterol, while if they get protein from meat they will notably raise it.

Another reason to stay away from meat consumption is the loads of chemicals and pathogens that may be inadvertently consumed along with it. Gary and Steven Null, in their book *Poisons in your Body,* say, "The animals [to be consumed] are kept alive and fattened by continuous administration of tranquilizers, hormones, antibiotics, and 2,700 other drugs. The process starts before the birth and continues long after death. Although these drugs will still be present in the meat when you eat it, the law does not require that they be listed on the package" (qtd. in "Dangerous Chemicals in Meat"). It is disgusting to think that by eating meat you are putting so many inorganic compounds in your body. Meat can also contain many pathogenic microorganisms that cause disease and infection. Recent outbreaks of foot and mouth disease and salmonella are reminders of the dangers involved in eating meat. Clearly there are some micro-organisms in plant foods, too, but they exist nowhere near in number and danger to human health as those found in meat.

Widespread consumption of meat is also wasteful and hurtful to the environment, and it carries economic consequences in terms of food production efficiency. Raising cattle and other livestock is particularly wasteful. According to the United States Department of Agriculture, over ninety percent of all of the grain produced in America goes to feed livestock — cows, pigs, sheep and chickens that wind up on dinner tables. This use of grain is extremely wasteful, though. The U.S. Department of Agriculture figures show that for every sixteen pounds of grain to feed livestock we get only one pound of meat in return. Americans are wasting food by choosing an increasingly carnivorous diet. I say "Americans" in particular because in third world countries they do not have the sort of economy that enables food waste like we have here in the United States. In underdeveloped countries a person on average consumes 400 pounds of grain a year, mostly directly. In America or in European countries a person consumes about 2000 pounds of grain by feeding it indirectly to livestock first.

Additionally, the consumer is hurt by the consumption of meat in terms of his disposable income. During government spot checks of supermarkets in the eighties it was found that sirloin steak cost about four dollars a pound, while a substantial vegetarian meal would cost only two dollars a pound — half the cost. Moreover, pollution is another economic problem of meat. The heavily contaminated runoff and sewage from slaughterhouses and feedlots are major sources of pollution in rivers and streams. The production of livestock causes about ten times as much pollution as residential areas and three times as much as industry. The production and consumption of meat is economically irresponsible and wasteful.

Despite noteworthy economic and health problems associated with the consumption and production of meat, the reason I first became a vegetarian is because of moral and ethical issues. Animals are slaughtered in the billions to suit our lifestyle, and many believe that the slaughtering is done in a humane way. Law requires that animals be sedated or stunned before being slaughtered, but this law is often disobeyed. Frequently cows are put on conveyer belts, their throats are slit and sometimes they are even cut alive. Even worse, birds such as chickens can be excluded from the humane death law and are occasionally burned alive.

Aside from the issue of humane killing of animals is the question of whether we should be killing animals in the first place. Sure, there are animals in nature that are predators and animals in nature that are prey, but humans are above this system. We have the ability to reason. Leo Tolstoy said, "Man suppresses himself, unnecessarily, the highest spiritual capacity — that of sympathy and pity toward living creatures like himself — and by violating his own feelings becomes cruel...while our bodies are the living graves of murdered animals, how can we expect any ideal conditions on earth" ("Famous Vegetarians"). I feel that if we have the ability to sustain ourselves by methods other than the killing of lower beings, then it is our duty to do so. Moral progress can only be made on this earth with the respect for the sentiment of life, not just for fellow man, but for animals, as well.

Vegetarianism is a higher form of living and a means to a more benevolent end. The human race would greatly improve if we could respect not only the lives of each other but also the lives of the animals that are among us. As Thoreau says in *Walden*, "I have no doubt that it is a part of the destiny of the human race, in its gradual improvement, to leave off eating animals, as surely as the savage tribes have left off eating each other when they came in contact with the more civilized" ("Quotes by Famous Vegetarians").

Works Cited

Dasa, Adiraja. "Vegetarianism: A Means to a Higher End." <http://www.webcom.com/~ara/col/books/VEG/hkvc1.html>.

"Different Types of Vegetarians." *Living Vegetarians: A Healthy Way to Eat.* <http://www.jtcwd.com/vegie/types.html>.

"Famous Vegetarians." *EATVEG.COM* <http://www.eatveg.com/peopleFamousVegetarians.htm#Historical%20Vegetarians%20&%20Advocates%20of%20Vegetarianism>.

Hoffman, Mary L. and Frank T. "Letter to The McAlvany Health Alert Concerning 'Healthy Heart.'" The Mary T. and Frank L. Hoffman Family Foundation and Allcreatures.org Letters and Responses. *All-Creatures.org.* <http://www.all-creatures.org/letters/mcalvany-16mar2002.html>.

"People—List by Firstname." *FamousVeggie.com.* <http://www.famousveggie.com/peoplenew.cfm>.

"Quotes by Famous Vegetarians." *FamousVeggie.com.* <http://www.famousveggie.com/quotes.cfm>.

Singer, Peter. *Animal Liberation.* Harper Collins, 2002.

"Dangerous Chemicals in Meat." *Vegetarian Life.* <http://www.skcv.com/vegetarian1.htm>.

"This is a Different Kind of War."

John Brophy

"This is a different kind of war" is a phrase many people are familiar with as the identifying phrase of the Vietnam War, the war that split the conscience of America. The many protesters against that war almost equaled the number of young men sent to a distant country. After the September 11th bombing, those words were again used, but by a different president in a different time. When George W. Bush told the millions of viewers at home that "this is a different kind of war," they applauded him ("President: We're Making Progress"). The presidential opinion polls showed that the American people had a 90% confidence rate in their president, an unprecedented showing for a leader whose election was less than awe-inspiring. The overwhelmingly positive response scared me.

What if in the remainder of our lives every president is in a constant state of war against regimes that do not support us? What lengths will we go to stop terrorism? Recently, a Taliban POW camp was bombed during an attempted insurgence and all of the prisoners were killed. Americans saw this event as just. There are reasons terrorists attack us, and there are reasons third world nations don't like us. George W. Bush, like his predecessors before him, has waged war without knowing exactly why. To the American people, the reason Bin Laden bombed us is because he is against freedom and democracy. To take this at face value is kidding ourselves. While his act was terrible, instead of only looking at terrorist actions, maybe it might help to look at the causes.

Since the very first regimes, terrorists have used violence as a way of getting attention for their causes. In Ireland, a band of terrorists under the command of now-war-hero, Michael Collins, killed many officers in the English crown's army to help the cause of Irish independence. Today Osama Bin Laden is the primary terrorist of note, but from the many people I've asked, no one seems to know the reason behind his attacks. This lack of awareness comes from today's press focus on the gory pictures and lasting TV images that only spread terror and confusion, without knowledge of what the terrorists are protesting.

I agree that Bin Laden must be brought to justice and that the Taliban regime is fascist in nature. But the reason Bin Laden and other terrorists do these things isn't simply to perform acts of bloodthirsty maniacs. Most nations don't like us. Many third world countries call us the "Great Devil" behind our backs. Why is this? Because our companies exploit their cheap labor, our government forces them into undesirable trade tariffs and, during the course of their existence, many countries have seen the United States provide money and weapons to oppressive governments to maintain the status quo.

Are these "wars of freedom" we carry out? The American human rights record in other countries is terrible. With regard to our current president's comment that Saddam gasses his own people, how many people did Bush execute in Texas? And our abuses go far beyond our borders. Many of the regimes hostile to us now we helped put in power. Bin Laden was trained in the School of Americas. There is strife in Ecuador and Columbia under dictatorships whose troops we trained. It seems like some of these nations would be better off without our interference.

Of course, our interference in any foreign situation is backed by one of two reasons: power or money. In Nicaragua, before the completion of the Panama Canal, the Nicaraguan government wouldn't let the United States finish the canal. So the United States incited a revolution in Panama and the first action of the new Panama government was to sign a deal with American contractors. Saddam Hussein had persecuted the native northern people of Iraq, the Kurds, for years while the United States did nothing. But when Kuwait was attacked and our precious fossil fuels were at stake, we quickly sent in the cavalry.

Our government, like many others before it, has waged war to protect its economic investments in other parts of the world. This isn't necessarily wrong, and in some instances innocent people were helped. But let's call them what they are: wars of economic investment. We are not defending political freedom, but laissez-faire capitalism. And this is why most non-Americans hate us and call us the "Great Devil." And how does the government react to the September 11th attack? Buy more, be an extreme capitalist. Be greedy…for your country. That is becoming the culture of America: secularism, materialism and consumerism. We are defined by our "stuff." And the only way to keep our stuff is to stay at the top.

The poorest people in America are doing much better than most of the populations of third world countries. Today, instead of certain groups of rich people, it's certain rich countries. These problems we cause seem distant and easily fixable with small donations to charities: "Your quarter will pay for twenty-two school books, eight vaccinations and three months of food for a village." Our corporations still use children in foreign factories to make our sports balls and expensive clothes, which we have known about for years. Some foolish people claim, "they don't have to take the job if they don't want it." It is not a matter of wants but needs. They don't live in America, and there isn't a help-wanted sign in every window. Our government forces other countries into low tariffs so their industries can't produce goods cheap enough to come anywhere near ours. And where do these unemployed people turn, but to the new Nike® factory that just opened and will pay them the generous sum of, say, five cents an hour. How nice of us. The new global economy is like a pyramid food chain with the same lion at the top, and the same ants getting squashed at the bottom. The whole aim of America's open market is to eventually dominate everyone else's economy.

What can we do? Write letters to our congressman, and tell our government not to support tyrannical leaders just because those tyrants guarantee the safety of American companies abroad. Tell Nike® to keep the shoes at $150 a pair, but to give more to the workers. I love America, and am proud to say that I live here, for if I lived somewhere else I could possibly be arrested for writing this. But the fact remains: as a human race, we have to look out for each other.

Works Cited

"President: We're Making Progress." *The White House*. 1 Oct. 2001. <http://www.whitehouse.gov/news/releases/2001/10/20011001-6.html>.